MW01164957

HELLO, HEAD, MEET HEART

HELLO, HEAD, MEET HEART

HOW TO TAP INTO YOUR EXTRAORDINARY LIFE

BY HANNAH MORGAN AUSTIN

NEW DEGREE PRESS

COPYRIGHT © 2023 BY HANNAH MORGAN AUSTIN

All rights reserved.

HELLO, HEAD, MEET HEART

How to Tap into Your Extraordinary Life

ISBN   979-8-88504-443-1 *Paperback*
        979-8-88504-466-0 *Ebook*

To my parents, thank you for teaching me to have roots and wings. And to Peter, thank you for loving me along the journey.

~H

CONTENTS

———

*"My barn having burned down;
I can now see the moon."*

—MIZUTA MASAHIDE
(SEVENTEENTH-CENTURY JAPANESE
POET AND SAMURAI)

INTRODUCTION

In the early Fall of 2020, I hit the darkest moment of my life and I was contemplating ending it all. I was supposed to be getting ready for work, but I could not get up from the bathroom floor. After another restless night of sleep, I had stumbled into the bathroom and folded onto the floor. I lay sprawled on my left side wearing my black and white Target pajama set from the night before, my warm cheek resting against the cold black hexagonal tiles. I cried silently, drowning in exhaustion and fatigue, as my body was beginning to fall apart.

A few weeks before, I felt the darkness coming over me like a heavy weighted blanket. Most days it was a struggle to get out of bed and get going. My heart felt like a rusty engine in a '52 pickup, just barely igniting only to catch and then rumble to a slow sustained hum. Once I was finally able to get up, I showered and dressed and put on my fake smile: ta-da! The quick-witted, strong career woman appeared on the Zoom stage. I was not the understudy; I was the lead actor, and I had perfected my role.

From the outside looking in, I had it all—a wonderful husband, a successful career, and a supportive network of family and friends. But inside I felt empty, depleted, and helpless. Since the start of COVID, I had been working from home and I missed my old life. I was lonely, isolated, and scared. I was tired of living each day like it was Groundhog Day and going through the motions. With no external forces at play any longer due to the imposed rules of the pandemic, I was forced to confront the poor physical and emotional state I was in and examine who I was as well as what I truly wanted. This was new territory for me, and I was terrified.

Two months later, on my day off, I experienced severe chest pain and drove myself to the hospital by where I worked. I was near collapse as I could feel the flames of stress and trauma beginning to scorch me. A few weeks later at work and after a tough conversation with my husband, I decided to walk away from a twenty-year successful career to save myself.

After I resigned, I decided to take the next few months off to heal my physical body and reignite my exhausted heart, mind, and soul. As I embarked on my new journey, I began to ask myself deeper questions. What was happening to me? How did I get here?

Not knowing where to start, I began googling my symptoms, researching what the heck was wrong with me.

Countless articles and studies stated that before the pandemic, just 5 percent of employed workers and 7 percent of unemployed workers said their mental health was poor or very poor. Now, mid-pandemic, 18 percent of employed and 27 percent of unemployed workers were saying they were struggling with mental health issues (Flex Jobs 2021).

I was floored. These statistics proved I wasn't crazy, and I wasn't alone. The data was staggering: 67 percent of all workers believe burnout had worsened throughout the pandemic (Indeed 2021). Then I read that the World Health Organization recognized burnout as a chronic condition (World Health Organization 2019). I was shell-shocked. I needed help. We all did. This was bigger than me.

As a natural fixer, I went into "fixer" mode. I started talking with people and interviewing them about the state of their mental health. I found they too were suffering from burnout, but they didn't know what to do or how to break through the cycle. As their stories unfolded, many of them shared the belief if they changed jobs, their burnout would go away. They felt stuck because they didn't know what their options were, and they were living an ordinary life filled with overwhelm and exhaustion, which they assumed was the only option for them. They also believed they could just "think" their way out of their burnout. But when I asked them, "Are these tactics working for you?" The overwhelming response was, "No."

The impact of COVID-19 had made it painfully clear our societal vision of burnout as a situational work-related condition wasn't accurate. Burnout wasn't going to go away overnight, and we were still knee-deep in the thick of it all.

I began to think we needed a bigger movement around this topic. If burnout was such a big issue, what were individuals and organizations actively doing about it? I believed we were thinking too small. We needed to address the issue with a multi-pronged approach. We needed to look at it from a new lens.

A spark ignited inside me. What if we could learn not only to heal from burnout but instead break through and thrive in our lives post-burnout? I asked myself: *What if I could build a community to help others heal from burnout and rise from the ashes to live an extraordinary life? What if I started the movement?*

Two months after asking myself these questions, I lit the fire. I started a company focused on helping professionals learn *how* to heal from burnout—SheShatters, LLC. Six months later I launched an international wellness podcast called *She Burns with Hannah Austin*. Nine months later I launched an organizational wellness speaking and engagement platform, which helps transform organizations to foster healthier mental health environments. As a natural driver, I couldn't stop there, so to make a more significant global impact, I decided to share my story and write the book I had always dreamed of—*Hello, Head, Meet Heart*.

As I started to write *Hello, Head, Meet Heart* and research the current state of burnout in our world, I found the statistics had become worse. In the second half of 2021, Gallup reported almost half of US employees were actively searching for a job. This phenomenon was dubbed "The Great Resignation" (Lighthouse 2022).

According to a recent article from Limeade, one of the biggest reasons for people quitting their jobs was feeling overwhelmed by work (Limeade 2022).

- A 2021 survey from Indeed found a 9 percent jump in employee burnout compared to pre-COVID numbers (Indeed 2021).
- Only 24 percent of employees surveyed in 2022 reported their company offered adequate support for them compared to 49 percent of workers satisfied with their employer support in 2020 (Limeade 2022).

It was clear the strategies companies and organizations were applying to tackle employee burnout weren't working. Because only 24 percent of workers felt their company offered adequate support for burnout prevention, I wanted to provide professionals with the tools to learn the "hows." How to ask for help, how to make a plan, how to have tough conversations with those you love, how to set boundaries, and how to overcome the biggest obstacle of all—doubt.

These skills allow my clients to rise from the ashes of burnout and help them rediscover a new version of themselves so they can live a life they love. Many of my clients believe they can self-care themselves out of burnout with a weekend at the beach or a massage, but I believe you cannot self-care your way out of burnout. My experience with clients and my burn-out has shown me that to beat burnout for good you need to get into your body, move from your head to your heart, and figure out why and how you burned out in the first place.

Hello, Head, Meet Heart is the next chapter in the movement to help professionals learn how to align their heads with their hearts. If you've struggled with feeling like you are failing at work or wasting your talents, or if you are simply looking for a new start and want to transition into a new role or a new career altogether, this book is for you.

I wrote this book for those of you reading this right now thinking, *I know there is more out there for me. I know deep down I am destined for more, but what is my "more"? And how do I find it? Hello, Head, Meet Heart* is for you if you're searching for something beyond the ordinary. Hopefully, as you read these pages you can feel my emotions, tears, and internal struggle as I searched for the answers to these complex life questions within myself. I hope by sharing my story and providing tools and exercises I can be of help to you on your journey.

As you read *Hello, Head, Meet Heart,* I want you to think about those times in your life when your dreams have bubbled up from your heart only to find them faded and buried in an avalanche of mind-numbing performances and to-do lists. How did your dream start? What did it feel like to live in an inspired heart space? How did it feel when your inspired high got slowly drowned out by stress and overwhelm?

Throughout the pages of *Hello, Head, Meet Heart*, you will hear about clients who have borne their hearts and souls by sharing their stories of burnout, resilience, courage, and hope.

Each chapter is designed to meet you where you are in your journey and to act as a blueprint you can follow, engage with, and participate in as you navigate your transition from burnout to living a fulfilling life. To help you on your way, most chapters include exercises and worksheet prompts designed to get you thinking and feeling things you may never have felt before. These thoughtful exercises developed through my work with colleagues and clients are designed for you to turn toward yourself so you can discover who you are and what you want your extraordinary life to be.

This isn't just a book; it's a journey, a way to find yourself. It's a map you can follow to connect your head and heart and guide you to the extraordinary life I know is within you. Know when you read this, I am right there by your side, cheering you on and whispering: "Take the leap. Take the risk. Don't settle for an ordinary life."

Take my hand, and together we will explore an extraordinary life.

CHAPTER 1

DEFINING MOMENT— THE PUSH AND PULL

"An open heart is an open mind."

—*DALAI LAMA XIV*

I am wasting my life. The first semi-conscious thought I could muster on a Monday morning. This statement had been my mind's mantra for months.

Since the pandemic began nine months earlier, my colleagues and I had been killing ourselves by working more than fifty hours a week. We were director-level executives at one of the largest healthcare companies in the country. We had spent the last nine months COVID-planning, building outside mini-hospitals, and executing worst-case scenarios. We had been in fight-or-flight mode, facing staffing shortages, lack of supplies with minimal breaks, no lunches, and triple-booked schedules with no relief in sight. Our boss Mary had been calling in sick frequently, and we needed a leader who was present. We were all feeling disconnected, and our leadership team was suffering because of it.

Sadly, I felt stuck in my job and had worked in my company long enough to know it would be career suicide to voice my concerns. This was not an option for me because I was tired of the corporate culture and, frankly, I just didn't have the energy for it anymore.

I would be turning forty-two in a few months and after twenty years in healthcare, I was burned out. I had been feeling unsettled for about a year before. I had been promoted, gotten a new title, gotten a pay raise, and had a flexible schedule. I was just overworked, overutilized, undervalued and so tired. I had lost my spark. The joke at my company was when you did great work and got great results, the reward was more work. It was a culture of golden handcuffs. We were paid extremely well, but we had become numb, shells of our former selves, which stifled the true innovation needing to come out. Once COVID hit, we were already emotionally drained and were operating on a net negative playing field.

As I sat at my desk in my home office, my Microsoft Team's icon began blinking as my coworker Daniel messaged me. "Did you see Mary called out sick?" My heart sank, and frustration bubbled up inside me. My boss called out sick again—on Monday and a day we were shifting new COVID workflows.

I put my head down on my desk and took a deep breath. Tears began to prick my eyes. Frustration, anger, disappointment, and a sense of dread came over me—an all-too-familiar feeling for the last nine months. My husband came into the room and saw me with my head down on the desk crying. I looked up at him. "I can't do this anymore. I am just done. I am just *so* done."

He took one look at me and said, "Oh, babe, what happened? I am so sorry. Okay, just be done. We will make it work."

So, I did. I resigned the next week. I left a six-figure director job at one of the most credible healthcare companies in the country to save myself.

THE DEFINING MOMENT

Many of us during COVID were blindsided by something out of our control. A virus infected our world. We felt helpless, scared, and fearful every day. Not knowing what would happen next, we were glued to our TVs and phones.

Throughout my interviews with hundreds of people, their stories revealed the many ways life can deliver an earth-shattering blindside: the loss of a job, your spouse telling you they have three months to live, receiving your own poor health diagnosis, your partner asking for a divorce, challenges with family or kids, a death. These are all life-defining moments.

One of the biggest betrayals of all, however, is the blindside you do to yourself by simply neglecting yourself, your needs, and your dreams while failing to listen to the voice inside you.

My blindside forced me to ask myself, *How could I ignore my own needs for so long?*

I kept turning a blind eye to what I was looking at in the mirror every day. I was gaining weight. I had just been diagnosed with high blood pressure and put on a blood pressure supplement. My body was falling apart. I had bruises, I had headaches, and I was hungry all the time. I was tired all the time. But I continued to push through until the day in the hospital when my body almost gave out. It had betrayed me. I had betrayed myself.

Many of the clients and colleagues I spoke with and interviewed for *Hello, Head, Meet Heart*, described their blind side as a pivotal moment when life smacked them across the face. Life said to them: "This isn't working for you anymore. Your relationship isn't working. Your health isn't working. Your husband is dying." It's a pivotal moment when life says, "Stop and see what's right in front of you."

When you're blindsided, you have several options. You can choose to accept it and move forward, shedding your former life and old patterns. This is often the most difficult choice but one with the biggest reward. Or you can revert to old patterns and move backward, making excuses for why you can't move on.

We often get stuck in the second bucket and don't know how to move forward because we are paralyzed from the blindside and terrified of what the future could bring. We are scared to get out of our heads, and we stay stuck in the ordinary. We fail to see what's possible for us. We fail to see the extraordinary.

To begin healing from a blindside, you must consciously choose to move forward. You must recognize the blindside you've experienced has now drawn a line in the sand, and you must choose which side of the line you want to stand on.

When faced with the decision of which side of the line to stand on, my colleague Matt stated, "Living an extraordinary life is a choice—a mind-set. You can choose to make a difference in your life, and you can choose to be happy." Matt chose to take a big leap and start a home design business he had been dreaming about for years. The design company had been his passion project on the side for years, but he wanted it to be more. He wanted to follow his heart and live fully in his dream instead of just having it as an accessory to the ordinary life he was living.

My crash-and-burn moment put an end to my ordinary life. A piece of me died on the bathroom floor and then again when I walked away from my twenty-year career, but it allowed me to stop, reflect, and ask myself: *Is this the life I want, or is it just an ordinary life?*

Based on the Oxford Dictionary's online edition, "ordinary" is described as commonplace or standard; I don't mean to downplay an ordinary life. In fact, before COVID, I was living one. But I was playing it safe, and I wasn't challenging myself. My life didn't fuel the flame inside of me any longer.

Because of this fact, I had to ask myself some tough questions:

1. Is my fear getting in the way of what I am truly capable of?
2. Is this all there is to life?
3. Is the work I'm doing fulfilling?
4. Is this the work I want to be doing?

As I look back now at the moment on the bathroom floor, the universe was telling me, "Get up and dance! This is your moment. You aren't done with this life. You can do more. You can do it." It got to the point where the voice was so loud it would wake me up at 2 a.m., 4 a.m., and 6 a.m. before I even got out of bed. In those quiet moments, I would ask myself: *Is there more to life than this?* I knew deep down there was.

Although I knew in my heart there was more to life than what I was currently experiencing, I didn't know what that something more was, and I didn't know how to start moving toward it.

THE PUSH AND PULL
As I began to unpack why I felt unfulfilled, I realized I had felt torn between the "work Hannah" (my head) and the "home Hannah" (my heart) for so long.

In our modern world, we often feel immense pressure to perform and be successful. We are pushed to perfection while at the same time feeling pulled in a different direction because our heart doesn't feel happy. We feel something is missing. This creates a push-pull relationship between our heads and our hearts. On the bathroom floor, my heart broke open. The ordinary life I was living wasn't working for me any longer, and I needed to find a way to truly follow my heart and design a life that would enable me to align all parts of myself.

For me to move forward, I had to learn how to create alignment in a practical, sustainable way. I needed a way to link my purpose and prosperity to live the extraordinary life I was seeking—a life I would love.

As I began to explore what an extraordinary life could look like, I began to feel a spark in me I'd never felt before. I began to be curious and excited. Lit up from the inside out, I almost felt like I was on fire, in a good way. I began to come up with incredible ideas—a company I could form and innovative product ideas. I could feel my dreams starting to take shape. I felt like I was living life in Technicolor when I had only known life in black and white. The world had never seemed so big, and I felt like I was finally taking up the space in it I was destined for. All the pieces of me finally locked into place. I was in my body again. My heart and my mind were all in alignment and pointing to my North Star to live an extraordinary life.

Ironically, where I had my crash-and-burn moment on the bathroom floor was the same place where I started dreaming about what could be. I don't know if it was the universe, God, or whoever telling me what I was destined for, but one morning in the shower, my inner voice said to me: *You need to start a company to empower people and share your story with them. You need to find out why professionals are burning out and help them with the tools necessary to keep them alive.*

I was confused because I didn't know who was in the bathroom with me or who was in the shower stall. I just knew I needed to listen to this voice.

I had heard this voice one other time in my life when the universe told me to get up. I had just completed college and struggled to find a job. This same voice made me get up and start charging forward on a road with no planned destination. Two weeks later I got the job of my dreams at the age of twenty-three.

This time, when I got out of the shower, and I started talking with my husband about what I experienced, we started brainstorming. I could create my own company, and I could support professionals like me. I wasn't an expert by any means in this area. But I knew my journey, my truth, and I was in the process of discovering how to save myself. The moment I decided to create an LLC, I felt a weight lifted off my shoulders. I felt like something was propelling me forward for the first time. It was scary and terrifying, but it was also exciting at the same time. I knew it would be extraordinary.

When I started to write *Hello, Head, Meet Heart*, and I told people the topic was about *how* to tap into your extraordinary life, several people asked me: "What's wrong with living an ordinary life?"

I paused. "Good question," I responded. "Nothing is wrong with living an ordinary life. Until your ordinary life becomes unhealthy for you and comes crashing down. If your ordinary life is no longer an option for you, then what?"

One of the biggest themes I've heard throughout my life is people do what they've always done because it's comfortable and because things have always been done that way. Often when someone breathes new ideas into their life or relationships, people immediately resist the change because the unknown scares them.

I think many of us fear leaping and reaching for more because we're afraid we will be let down or disappointed. We are scared to fail. We cannot see the capabilities we have within us to do more. We are busy in our lives, and we don't stretch ourselves to see what's outside of our current view. We think our job or day-to-day life is the only way to do it. We think too small for ourselves, and we don't take the time to stop, explore, and find out what is or what could be out there for us.

No matter what the defining moment is in your life, this is your moment to stop and assess. Check in with yourself and take the time to rest, heal, and examine what's next for you. This is an opportunity for you to turn toward yourself and look into your heart.

You may be thinking this all sounds great, but *how* do I rest and take the time to check in with myself with so many competing priorities in my life? Turn ahead to chapter 2 where we will examine *how* you got to a place of burnout and *why*. We will more deeply explore those key traits and patterns in your life, which are showing up for you and have contributed to your defining moment.

CHAPTER 2

HOW DID I GET HERE? THE SIX SELVES

"You have to take better care of yourself. It is just a job. Why are you killing yourself?" Two months after finding myself on the bathroom floor, I was in the hospital. The attending doctor's question stopped me cold.

This pivotal conversation with the doctor made me ask: *Why was I working so hard? What was the purpose? What was this obsession with work, other than a paycheck?* I was feeling so depleted, useless, lost, and tired. And I didn't like who I was. I didn't know who I was anymore.

When I think back to how I wound up on the bathroom floor, and then in the hospital, I realized it all started for me at the age of three.

When I was three years old, my father abandoned my mom and me to live a new life, and I watched my mom work two jobs for us to survive. After my biological father left, my mom went into "everything mode," and she had a distinct order to her priorities. She always put me first, work second, and herself last.

The patterns of my mom's priorities subconsciously validated to me that as women we were to put everyone and everything before ourselves. I always respected and admired my mom as a career woman. She was a role model for me. A few years later when my mom met my soon-to-be stepdad, hard work was again validated. He was a Harvard graduate and had a type A-minus personality. In our new household, they encouraged excellence.

Being an only child, my parents spent a lot of time focusing on me and helping to shape me into the best human, woman, and student I could be. The pressure was always there. The pressure to make them proud. The pressure to do not only my best but to achieve and be rewarded. I was raised in the middle class, and I was raised to work hard, but I was also raised to give back to my community.

Seeing both my parents exhibit these traits created a foundation in me for what was to come. As I achieved, I wanted more. And as I excelled, I kept pushing my boundary line. I liked the feeling of setting a goal, achieving it, and moving on. Looking back, I realize I never stopped to appreciate and acknowledge my hard work. I was always looking for what was next.

In my senior year in college at Oregon State University, I applied for an "administrator in training" role at a reputable senior care facility in Portland. After a long and vigorous interview process, I was notified I got the internship. Once I secured the AIT position, my healthcare administration journey began. A year later, after 980 hours of practical experience and sitting for the Nursing Home Administrator Board exam and passing, I was ready to apply for my first job making a real salary.

At the age of twenty-three, I interviewed for a job as a marketing director with a senior housing company. During the interview, the manager interviewing me said, "You are interviewing for the wrong job. We're going to make you the executive director instead of the marketing director."

He saw something in me I didn't see, and the decision propelled me forward quickly into my career. A month later I found myself managing the largest assisted living facility in the state of Oregon. I had over fifty staff reporting to me, and I had *no* clue what I was doing. I quickly learned I needed to figure it out. I learned to fake it on the outside and never let anyone know I was Googling, taking classes on the side, and doing everything I could to figure out on my own how to succeed.

I excelled in the role, and then two years later I was promoted to another job that stretched me again as a leader. With the promotion, I got more money and more responsibility. Receiving the promotion validated that what I was doing behind the scenes was working. So, I continued to do it again year after year after year.

The first time I burned out was two years later when I was twenty-five years old. I began having chest pains at work. I went to the doctor, and they diagnosed me with something called costochondritis, which means inflammation of the chest wall and that my heart was beating too fast. I had so much anxiety, my heart was struggling to keep up.

A year later, I wound up in the emergency room with gallbladder issues, and I had to get my gallbladder surgically removed. After surgery I sought alternative medical care from a Chinese medicine doctor. I asked the doctor, "What is the gallbladder used for?" And he replied, "It is designed to filter out and process anger."

Because I had pushed myself so hard, I was storing my unreleased anger inside me. The gallbladder blockage was a sign signaling to me to release the anger and old patterns. My body was telling me to take a break and let go.

In reflection for the last fifteen years, my body has been telling me to take a break in a variety of ways. Whether via a car accident, falling off a ladder, or being clumsy by running into things my body was telling me, "Stop, and pay attention. You are not alert. You are not in your body. Where are you?"

The map of bruises on my body was signaling to me to stop, slow down, and find myself. At the moment, I just thought I was clumsy, so I kept moving. But the reality was I wasn't living a conscious life.

As I approached my early thirties, I began to dream of a bigger career, a bigger arena. I decided to get my MBA. I worked a full-time job as I pursued my MBA. At the age of thirty-two, during the last few months of my MBA program, my husband had a stroke. And just as my mother did when my father left us, I went into "everything mode." Once again, my health took a back seat, and so did I.

Once I got my MBA, I thought, *I'm done. I've reached the highest level.* But then I inched the boundary line higher again. My next goal was to become a COO of a major healthcare organization. Once I became a manager and then a director within the same organization, I began to look around at all of the women around me who were COO and CEO.

I realized what they had to sacrifice to get there. I watched them daily. They had to put on an act and stand up in front of the crowd. They had to toot the horn and drink the Kool-Aid.

As I watched them, I thought: *Is this truly who I am? Do I believe what I'm saying?* I started to question the CEO and COO, and then I started questioning my chosen path. The COO and CEO life didn't look so shiny to me anymore, but when I thought about what I wanted in my career during this difficult time, I realized I had never created a contingency plan for myself. What was my backup plan if the dream I thought I wanted wasn't what I wanted anymore?

It became clear to me I had swallowed the story of success like so many of us in society have. Our society tells us to "look and be like them," "strive for promotions," and "make more money." Our society does not reward unique or different. It doesn't promote *being* or *feeling*. It rewards doing, productivity, and outcomes.

What we have seen happening recently with the Great Resignation and an increase in burnout shows us that the "should" mentality isn't working for employees and workers any longer. Employees are tired of the old reward system and of being burned out. According to Indeed, 52 percent of employees feel burned out (Gul 2022). This suggests more than half of the workforce is struggling with managing their work-life balance and struggling with burnout.

The question is how do you start to heal from burnout once you identify you are in it? I suggest you start with where you are right now and do a deep dive into what patterns got you to a place of burnout.

THE SIX SELVES

My story isn't unique. Most of my clients at one point found themselves in the same position: high-achieving and successful but burned out and overwhelmed. And most of them didn't have a contingency plan because they never imagined another life for themselves.

In my discussions with hundreds of professionals throughout my journey, I have identified *Six Selves* many of us fall into, or we are a combination of a few of them. These traits may be how you've gotten your success up until this point, but if you continue to lean into these traits, they are also the primary reason why you may be feeling depleted or stuck. I call them the *Six Selves*.

The first self is the *people pleaser*. The people pleaser loves to make other people happy. Oftentimes they will lose themselves in their quest to please others, but they continue to do it because all that matters is that "they" are happy.

The second self is the *perfectionist.* They love to do it the right and perfect way. They *need* to get it right. Oftentimes the perfectionist will work on things for hours, overthink emails they send, or replay conversations in their heads. They worry they will get it wrong.

The third self is the *over-functioning self.* The over-functioning self is the strong one, the one who holds it all together and who always says, "I'll do it," when anything needs to be done. They pretend they can do it alone. They don't ask for help as they see it as a weakness. They take it on all by themselves, and ultimately, this leads to burnout because they are doing way more than any one person can or should do. It is their identity. They know nothing else.

The fourth self is the *helper.* The helper often gets their worth and defines their value by being useful to other people. They will jump in to help others, oftentimes abandoning themselves in the process. So many women and men fall into this category, and often once we have kids, it gets worse.

The fifth self is the *overachiever.* This ambitious self was always striving for the next accomplishment, always running the race. Once they achieve their goal, the bar gets set even higher. There's no "enough" for the overachiever.

Lastly, the sixth one is the *nice person.* The nice one is always pleasant and pretends to be easy and flexible in an attempt to not rock the boat. They pretend they are always okay. They build up resentment, and inside they are secretly really angry. And then one day they may explode at the people they love the most.

As you read through these categories, you may find you strongly see yourself in one of the buckets, or you could be a combination of two or three of them. You will want to consider how these interplay in your life. Here's an example. I see myself clearly in two buckets: the over-functioner and the overachiever.

My over-functioning nature stems from my high-functioning anxiety. For so many years I thought if I was the go-to person and could handle it all, I could control the turmoil going on inside me. The narrative was false. All it did was burn me out, and I still found myself increasingly anxious. The over-functioning propelled the overachiever in me as I worked harder. I was rewarded and achieved more but it was a vicious cycle as the rewards were external rewards, which led me to feel emotionally depleted.

One of the most common types of the Six Selves is the "helper." We see this type often in healthcare, education, and public service roles. An example of a helper is my client, Meredith. Meredith's story is all too familiar. She was referred to me during the mid-to-later part of the pandemic. She had been in the healthcare industry for over a decade and was feeling burned out, depleted, and emotionally abandoned after giving away so much of herself to her career, her husband, and two kids. During one of our sessions focused on the question of *how I got here,* she said, "I got so caught up in everyone else in my life, I forgot to look after myself. I had to take a leave of absence it was so bad, and now I know I need to adjust the areas that were priorities in my life before but aren't priorities now."

This was a great insight on Meredith's behalf. This recognition allowed her to identify the old patterns of behaviors that got her to this place of burnout and set the stage for the changes she wanted to make. This revelation also allowed her to focus on taking the next step toward exploring her options and finding her purpose.

Do any of these descriptions sound like you? Do you say yes when you want to really say no? Do you have a hard time setting boundaries? Do you have trouble speaking up for yourself at work or in a relationship? Does nothing ever feel like it's good enough? Do you doubt yourself? Do you have a hard time turning off your brain? Do you push yourself so hard and never slow down until your body crashes and burns?

If you responded with, "Hell, yes!" to any of these, you are not alone. Honestly, I could be president of the over-functioning club.

COPING MECHANISMS:
One of the biggest ah-has I had at the beginning of my recovery journey was diving deep into the coping mechanisms I had created in my life as I was in the thick of burnout. I was stuck in a never-ending cycle of overworking, which caused me to be depleted, which led me to make convenient but poor food choices. I ordered too many unhealthy and salty

foods, which led me to feel guilty and led to sleeping problems. I would wake up tired, and then I would drink coffee, which elevated my blood pressure and increased my heart rate, which caused me to have adrenal problems, weight gain, and headaches.

One year later in my career as a coach, many of my clients shared their stories of coping mechanisms: cutting themselves, drinking too much, obsessing over exercise, using sex as an outlet, and drug overuse. The list of coping mechanisms goes on and on but the important thing to know is we all have coping mechanisms, and they are all deeply personal. Do any of these coping mechanisms sound familiar to you? If so, you are not alone. You are one of the 63 percent of workers who believe work stress causes them to practice unhealthy behaviors (My Disability Jobs 2022).

As your journey unfolds, you will want to ask yourself, "Which of these selves do I fall into?" Examine those key traits and patterns in your life showing up for you. On the path to discovering who you truly are and want to be, you must shift, replace, and reorganize your intricate puzzle pieces in order to create a new puzzle. You have the choice and the power within you to rearrange and discard those pieces no longer working for you. Once you start to rearrange the pieces, your puzzle view will expand, which will leave space for you to carefully design and select new pieces to bring growth, joy, and beauty into your life. In chapter 3 we will explore how to do this.

CHAPTER 3

EXPLORING YOUR OPTIONS AND FINDING YOUR PURPOSE

"It doesn't interest me what you do for a living. I want to know what you ache for and if you dare to dream of meeting your heart's longing."

—ORIAH MOUNTAIN DREAMER

The moment I experienced on the bathroom floor and my near collapse in the hospital demonstrated I couldn't live this way anymore. Those moments of distress happened because I was trying to control everything. I was so afraid of what would happen if I let go.

The pivotal point for me to decide to leave my job, however, was my husband encouraging me to let go and "just be done." The permission he offered at that crucial moment made me realize I didn't need to make this decision alone; I had his support to make the choice to let go. When he said those three supportive words to me, I felt immense relief. But I also argued with him and said, "No, we need the money. I need to stay. I should be strong enough to work through this."

But as I began to verbally resist the offer of permission, even I didn't believe the words I was saying anymore. I no longer believed the lie I had been telling myself for two decades, and now was the time to stop the lie.

Once I started getting honest with myself, I still had a big hill to climb to unravel the lie I had been living. I had to unbundle all of the old patterns I had created. I found I had a lot of work to do to figure out new ways to be authentic with myself and get to know *who* I was without the job title and the career. As a woman without children, my whole life and identity were wrapped up in my job, and without my career, I needed to establish a new identity.

As I started to feel out what steps I needed to take to begin leaving my job, I started to craft in my mind what I wanted to say to people about why I was leaving. How honest did I want to be? I wanted to keep it professional, but I also needed to be authentic.

I began to share with close friends and family members that I had decided to quit my job and take some time to rest, recharge, and figure out what I wanted to do next. I had no plans. I didn't even know what I wanted to do. I just knew I planned to rebuild who I was again.

I began to turn on a new mantra which was, *I am betting on myself for the first time in my life.* I chose this mantra because I have always had a plan my entire life. This was the first time I was taking a leap of faith. And the only way I could justify the leap of faith in my mind was to trust myself enough to know I was going to be fine no matter what. So I rephrased it, *I am betting on myself.*

FIRST STEPS: ASKING FOR HELP

As my conversations unfolded with friends and family members, several people were skeptical and said, "What are you going to do for money? What are you going to do with your time? You're going to be bored in three days."

I made up my mind then and there. When I would start to second-guess my decision or start to agree with them, I was going to think about myself on the bathroom floor in a heap. I was going to keep looking back at the visual of the woman on the floor. And I was going to do whatever it took to get her up off the bathroom floor and keep her out of the hospital. Nothing could be worse than losing who you are or putting your health at risk. I had lost myself.

A question surfaced: If I wasn't living my life as me, who was living it?

Because I was so unsure of who had been living my life, I was scared I would relive old patterns and become a workaholic again. If I had been the one living my life without feeling a sense of control or clarity, I was on unstable ground. For the first time in my life, I didn't have a plan, which made me super uncomfortable, and I was terrified.

The terror would manifest itself through insomnia and small anxiety attacks throughout the day. I was wrought with worry. Worry I wasn't going to be able to find something else. Worry I made a mistake in leaving my old work life behind. Worry I would have to settle for something I didn't want.

I was in a cycle of mind-fucking myself to death, and I knew I needed help getting out of the cycle.

I reached out for help from my therapist, whom I trusted and had worked with for more than sixteen years. She suggested I hire a career coach. I wasn't sure I needed one, but as I began to speak with a few other women I trusted who had been through similar midlife work crises, one of them also suggested I explore a career coach. She said she had worked with one—Stacey—and she had experienced great results. I scheduled a meet and greet with Stacey the next day and ended up hiring her.

By hiring Stacey, I took another key step by reaching out for help. My meetings with Stacey were fairly scheduled and prescribed, which I appreciated. I felt like I was moving forward on my journey to deciding what was next. She helped me redo my résumé and update my LinkedIn profile. What she did with my résumé was incredible. I would have hired myself based on what she wrote about me!

During our sessions, she helped me realize I had been short-changing myself for many years. The organization I had worked for had created a golden handcuffs scenario where I was paid well, and I was led to believe I would not find anything better outside of my organization. Boy was I wrong. The amount of interest I experienced and the opportunities that arose were incredible.

I began applying for roles like VP and COO because it's what I thought I wanted. I had only looked at elevated roles offering more money and that came with more status. Never had I stopped and thought: *Do I want this?* But as I explored those opportunities, I found myself uninspired by the roles I was being recruited for. It was the same game, just a different company and players.

I began to panic. This didn't *feel* right. What was I going to do now? I went back to my therapist, and we discussed this. I shared with her that I thought something was wrong with me because I didn't feel like I could settle again for the same thing I'd always done. I felt a yearning and craving to get out of my comfort zone. Something inside me was saying to stretch higher, not toward a different role or a different industry, but stretch. Stretch yourself as you've never stretched before.

My client Allyson experienced a similar struggle as she started to explore her options. Allyson was working in HR and was bored out of her mind. Her dream was to be an actress and a musical playwright. She started writing a musical on the side while she continued her day job in HR.

Once the musical was finished and she started to begin the casting process, she received feedback three times that her musical read like a novel. It stopped her in her tracks as it was hard feedback for her to hear. She fought against it. She stopped writing for six months because she got so lost in the feedback she was given.

Then she decided to ask for help and hired a coach. By working through the fear and the pain with her coach, she began to lean into the feedback and started converting the musical into a novel. Eight months later she published her first novel. By listening to the feedback and leaning into the possibility of different options, Allyson was able to let go of what she thought needed to happen, push through her self-created boundaries, and instead trust in the feedback to believe in herself and turn the feedback into her new reality.

The new reality was better than she could have ever imagined.

FINDING THE PATH

Sometimes working from an outside lens or different perspective is the key to opening those doors you never even knew existed. Knowing I was searching for what was next, and I was ready for the challenge, my therapist gave me an assignment. I was to research women I admired in the world. She wanted me to make a list of those women, what they had accomplished, and why I admired them. I was excited and up for the task because it was different. It wasn't the same old thing of stalking someone on LinkedIn and applying for a job. I was actively searching out qualities I admired, not just those that were well-known.

The assignment forced me to tweak my previous approach. It switched me from thinking to feeling and moved me from my head to my heart. I began to realize there was more for me out there than just another role and just another title. If I wanted to truly create movement or make a change, I had to think bigger and more expansive than I ever had before.

As I began to explore and research articles, TED talks, and books about these inspiring and incredible women, something inside me began to unlock, and a few pieces started to rearrange themselves. I began to stretch my outlook and think about my options and possibilities.

I pondered: *What if I took all of my decades of experience, coupled with what I yearned for, and put my experience into action? What if the CEO role I wanted was actually to become the CEO of my own company and create a movement of hope for other professionals who have been through what I had?*

Guiding women and professionals to unlock their potential before it's too late. Encouraging them to shift from their ordinary to their extraordinary. I began to get excited. I began to start dreaming about the names of my company, dreaming of logos, and researching what it would take to start a company. I talked with anyone and everyone who would talk with me about how they started their company, why they started it, and what pitfalls to watch out for.

The questions bubbled up. Was this something I was a good fit for? To fully vet the answer, I needed an outside lens again. What couldn't I see about myself? Was I thinking too small, or was the old doubt too big?

To answer this question, my coach and I came up with an idea to reach out to some of my most trusted colleagues and previous support systems. The plan was to ask them from their perspective. What was I good at, and what did they see me doing? I sent each of them an email asking them for their feedback.

I asked them three questions:

- *What adjectives would you use to describe me?*
- *What would you describe as my professional reputation?*
- *If you could think of an ideal job for me, what would it be? Or what would it be like?*

The responses I received were heartwarming. The adjectives they used to describe me were incredible, passionate, progressive, compassionate, warm, wise, driven, and a change agent. They described my perfect role as one that would channel my passion to serve and be movement and mission based—a role that promoted strong output outcomes and demanded equity and ethical practices.

By completing this exercise, I felt like my internal dialogue combined with the external feedback I received locked something into place for me. It couldn't have been clearer. The answer was there all along. I was born to drive, facilitate, and serve others.

Reaching out to your trusted friends, family, and colleagues and asking them questions provides you with more data points for you to add to your "explore your options" bucket. It also provides you with a new lens to look through.

One of the biggest roadblocks that can dull your imagination is not seeing yourself for who you truly are. So many times I said to myself: *Who am I to leave a twenty-year career behind? Who am I to try and live an extraordinary life? Am I deserving of living an extraordinary life? Is it okay to ask for more? Why couldn't I just be happy with what I had? The career and life I had were what so many people dreamed of. Why couldn't enough just be enough?*

So many of us are afraid to unlock our potential. We feel guilty, and we are scared to be more deserving.

This was true in my case. I was trying to *think* about what living an extraordinary life was instead of *feeling* what an extraordinary life was. Mariah, my therapist asking me to complete the assignment of researching women I admired, shifted me from my head to my heart. And that's when things fell into place for me. I clearly saw and felt it. When you *see* a woman living an extraordinary life, she sets the example that you are worthy because she is worthy, and it is not only okay to reach for more, it is your destiny.

START WITH ONE STEP

Once you've begun to explore your options, now is the time to discover what your extraordinary is.

My colleague Lisa says, "If I were to tell people where to start in breaking through burnout and beginning to live an extraordinary life, I would tell them, 'You start with a few small steps.'" Lisa recommends completing the below exercise as the first step.

YOUR EXTRAORDINARY EXERCISE:

- Grab two pieces of paper. On one piece of paper, write down absolutely everything you know about yourself, things only you would know.
- Now on the other piece of paper, write down everything you think other people know about you. And if you don't know what they know, ask them.
- Once those steps are completed, place both papers side by side.
- Ask yourself what's the difference between the two pieces of paper. You might be surprised people know more about you than you think you know about yourself.
- Then incorporate both lists together onto one piece of paper. The single list is your extraordinary. It's *you.*

Lisa summarized this exercise saying: "Who you are is now on one piece of paper. Whenever you doubt yourself, get the piece of paper out, and you'll know your talent and unique blueprint. Then start squirreling away enough money so you have three months' worth of wages sitting there and give your talent a chance. Know you are employable because there's your talent. The piece of paper is proof."

FINDING YOUR PURPOSE EXERCISES:

To continue on the road of finding your purpose, we must first examine the question: "What brings you joy?" This seems like a very simple question, but so many of my clients struggle with answering it, and it was difficult for me to answer at first as well. Not examining this question contributed to me losing myself. Not living my joy led me to burnout.

Take a few minutes and list a few things that bring you joy. Think about it in three buckets:

- What brings you joy at work?
- What brings you joy at home?
- What brings you joy in your heart?

So why did we complete the joy exercise? Finding joy in life leads you to understand why you are here on this planet and what causes your life to be sustainable, meaningful, and purposeful. Often when we are laser-focused on one thing, such as being a stay-at-home parent, being a caregiver, or focusing on our career, we can lose sight of *why* we started doing something in the first place.

This is very common. Life is distracting, and in stressful times, it is all too easy to tilt off course and get lost. So many of my clients say they don't know who they are anymore or what brings them joy, and this exercise is a great way to ground you and bring you home to yourself.

So now that we've explored what brings us joy, let's move on to the next step. I love this exercise and I ask my guests this question on season 1 of the *She Burns with Hannah Austin* podcast. It's called "Who Are You Really?" (Dutra-St. John 2009).

WHO ARE YOU REALLY?

To help you uncover what you must do, express, give, or experience at this point in your life, complete the following sentence five times without censoring yourself.

- If you really knew me, you would know that I...
- If you really knew me, you would know that I...
- If you really knew me, you would know that I...
- If you really knew me, you would know that I...
- If you really knew me, you would know that I...

Once you have completed the exercise, here are a few reflection questions for you:

1) What was the exercise like for you?

2) Did the question get harder as you answered it over and over?

3) Did anything new come up you didn't know about yourself?

Through these exercises, we created a space for you to become more self-aware. Self-awareness is all about looking inward, and here we can clarify and examine our values, thoughts, feelings, and behaviors. During many of my client sessions, we spend a lot of time working on the theme of creating "busyness" in our lives to avoid our true feelings. It is often much easier for us to go, go, go than to slow down and examine what is working and what isn't in our lives.

Why do we do this? It is scary to face our challenges. It takes work and it at times can be painful. But...when we don't, we see the same old patterns resurface, we burn out over and over again, we hurt ourselves and others repeatedly until we hit our breaking point, and then we are back to being stuck.

By giving ourselves permission to pause, turn inward, and ask ourselves thought-provoking questions, we can create a space for our souls to become re-energized and grow. This energy gives us hope and creates a spark that lights a fire within us. In the next chapter, you will learn about the concept of head and heart alignment. Learning *how* to align both will help you form a solid foundational roadmap for your journey ahead.

CHAPTER 4

HELLO, HEAD, MEET HEART

―

During my three-month post-resignation sabbatical, I decided to take a qigong exercise class at a retreat center in Arizona. As I walked through the campus toward the outside class, I saw a single man standing under a large weeping willow tree holding a roster clipboard. He was incredibly fit and beamed at me with a huge smile. It lit up his entire face.

"Hannah?" he asked cautiously.

"Hi, yes I'm Hannah," I replied.

He began to slowly walk toward me. "Wonderful. It's just going to be you and me today. Due to the pandemic, you were the only person signed up, so it will be a private session."

"Oh, wow! Go easy on me," I teased.

He threw his head back and roared with laughter as he spoke. "I like you already but from what I can tell I should ask you to go easy on me." He motioned for me to join him under the tree and set the roster clipboard down. He asked me to take off my shoes and socks, stand with my legs chest-width apart, and breathe in and out slowly.

How does this feel?" he said.

"Uncomfortable and boring," I responded. I knew I had to be honest with him and getting into my body was uncomfortable for me. I didn't like the discomfort because it unsettled me.

The instructor roared with laughter.

"Qigong is a system of coordinated body posture and movement, breathing, and meditation used for the purpose of opening certain energy gates and channels in your body. The term "qi" means "life force" and "gong" means "work or gather.""

"Hmmm-interesting," I replied. *How long is this session?* I wondered. He looked down at my feet, sensing my discomfort.

"Interesting," he said.

"What?" I asked.

"Do you see your left foot is barely touching the ground? You are perching yourself on the ball of your left foot."

I looked down. Yes, it looked like I was ready to bolt—a familiar stance for me.

"This signifies you are anticipating your next move, ready to run. Is this your typical stance?"

I responded truthfully, "Hmm, I hadn't noticed, but yes, you never know when something will happen, and I want to be ready to hit the ground running."

He nodded slowly and smiled softly with deep understanding in his eyes.

"I've been there, and I understand. I am here to help you breathe, feel the feelings, and ground yourself. Power lies in facing the feelings and not running from them. The growth happens as you breathe in and out, pushing the energy blockages away from your body and bringing the love and joy back toward your body."

He began to move his arms from his heart away from his body and exhaled. Then as he inhaled, he cradled his hands toward his body close to his heart. "Breathe with me," he said.

So, I did. We did this exercise continually in and out and in and out until I lost track of the time. My mind began to focus on what I wanted to push away from my life—the pressure and stress from my recent job, the loss of my identity, the fear of not bringing in any income, the fear of getting COVID, the sadness of not being able to see friends and family during the pandemic. I began to feel lighter and more grounded.

As I cradled my hand toward my body and close to my heart, I closed my eyes and visualized a brilliantly sunny day, sailing on the water with my husband by my side. My heart began to feel fullness, and slowly joy crept in as I smiled. I had not felt this feeling in a while, and it felt good.

Then another feeling came. I hadn't felt the feeling in a long time, but it was like seeing an old friend again. It was hope. My heart felt lighter, and I felt safe. I welcomed it inside me.

I looked down at my feet and saw my left foot was planted on the ground. I was rooted to the grass. I did not feel the need to run to the next thing. I was content.

"Ah," the instructor said, "you found it."

"Yes," I whispered back, "I did."

And I smiled.

Having the opportunity to take the qigong class at a retreat center was a blessing for me and a life-changing moment—a blessing I know not all people can afford. One of the promises and commitments I made to myself when I decided to start my company SheShatters was I wanted to share the resources and tools I had learned along my journey with others in this world without the steep and unaffordable price tag. One of the most valuable resources you can learn is to be introduced to your head and heart.

In working with my clients, the biggest surprise they have during our time working together is they are stuck in their heads. They are constantly in the cycle of "mind-fucking themselves." Our society has taught them to rely on the outside external world to validate them and has trained us to make our decisions based on comparison and judgment—not our internal compass and intuition.

Clients are referred to me after they've tried to "think" themselves out of burnout as what they've been taught all along from society didn't work. Because they were stuck, they couldn't even begin to grasp the bigger picture about what life could look like after their burnout and what an extraordinary life could be. To move past this toxic cycle, we talk a lot in our sessions about tapping into the internal self and introducing our head to our heart.

My client Meg describes her struggle with feeling torn between listening to her heart versus her head: "I convinced myself I was happy with who I was, but my head and heart knew they weren't aligned. I could convince myself I was happy enough to show people I was on the outside, but if I asked myself if my head and heart were aligned, I knew they weren't. And I think many of us know that inside. We just don't say it out loud."

In everyday life, logically it makes sense to problem-solve in our heads. Our society and educational pathways reinforce this. But our logical brain often holds us back and limits us. We can work through burnout and shift our focus by tapping into our extraordinary life while getting out of our heads and into our bodies and heart.

TAPPING INTO YOUR BODY

My client Ingrid is a great example of someone who struggles with grasping the concept of moving out of her head and into her body. Ingrid is an IT manager for an international start-up. She is an intelligent, analytical woman who was trained most of her life to rely on facts and data when making decisions in her work and personal life. During our first session, I asked her what she would like to focus on during our time together. She said, "I feel like a part of me is missing. I feel numb sometimes."

During a few of our sessions, I taught Ingrid the concept of body scanning to tap and drop down into her body. Here is the exercise we used:

- Start by getting comfortable, possibly in a seated position. Close your eyes.
- Focus on your lower body. Notice how your feet feel on the floor. Slowly, move your attention to your ankles, knees, thighs, and then pelvis. Identify temperature, pressure, tension, and any other sensations as you move up your body.
- When you feel any tension, take a deep breath and exhale as you release it. When you feel the body part relax, you can move to the next one.
- When you finish with your lower body, do the same with your upper body. Include some of your internal organs like your stomach, heart, and lungs.
- Finally, end by focusing on your neck, head, and face.

This exercise allowed Ingrid to drop into her body, scan it for any sensations that bubbled up inside her, and get in touch with what she was feeling. In essence, she was paying attention and being conscious of the sensations her body was telling her. She was learning to listen to herself.

Because this was a new concept for her, she required several repeat sessions to practice this internal shifting. As Ingrid became more comfortable with the shift, we expanded to another exercise that reinforced the comfort and safety of following her internal senses.

The next progressive step touched on the concept of self-regulation. Clinical Social Worker Andrea Bell defines self-regulation as "control [of oneself] by oneself." Bell also states: "Someone who has good emotional self-regulation can keep their emotions in check. They can resist impulsive behaviors that might worsen their situation, and they can cheer themselves up when they're feeling down. They have a flexible range of emotional and behavioral responses that are well matched to the demands of their environment."

Here are some of the exercises Ingrid and I explored:

- Hug yourself. To do this, cross your right arm over your chest, placing your hand near your heart. Then, cross your left arm, placing your left hand on your right shoulder. This concept can make you feel contained, which may make you feel safe. Hold the hug for as long as you need.
- With your hand in a cupping position, tap your body all over, from your feet to your head. You can also try squeezing different parts of your body instead of tapping them. This will help you with grounding, but also help

your body recognize your boundaries, which can also give you a sense of being contained and safe.

After the self-regulation exercise, Ingrid shared with me she felt she found a new piece of herself she'd never known was there. Ingrid and I talked about the concept of learning to activate your mind, heart, and body in a synergetic way when making decisions. You do not have to choose one over the other. The head and the heart/body need to work together to allow your heart to set the vision and direction while your head guides you there through the use of data, action steps, and a plan.

Overall, tons of evidence suggest that those who success-fully display self-regulation in their everyday behavior enjoy greater well-being. According to Jack Kornfield, researchers Skowron, Holmes, and Sabatelli found greater self-regulation was positively correlated with well-being for both men and women (2021).

Kornfield says, "When we listen with the heart, beneath all the busyness of thought, we discover a sweet, healing silence, an inherent peacefulness in each of us, a goodness of heart, strength, and wholeness is our birthright. We discover the healing heart beyond the thinking mind."

THE SHOULDS
Choosing to abandon our heart and instead choose our head is a defense mechanism we often fall back on. It's scary to feel our emotions because sometimes the emotion isn't a good one. One of the most common examples of this is replacing

what you may want instead with what you "should" do. Listening to our "shoulds" is one primary way we disconnect ourselves from our bodies and our hearts.

An example of this dilemma showed up with my client, Karen, who came to me for support with overcoming her burnout. She had also been struggling with deep depression and had knee-deep angst with the "shoulds." During our first session together, we discussed what she would like to focus on. "I always do what is expected of me, what I *should* do and never what I want to do. I have ignored my feelings for so long I don't even know what they are anymore."

Karen wasn't alone in her quest to overcome the "shoulds." Karen had been raised in a religious setting that reinforced tradition, duty, and servitude. She had been taught in her formative years to be dutiful and outcome driven. Together in our sessions, we focused on tapping into her breath, focusing on her inner voice, and vocalizing her wants and needs.

Here is an example of one of the exercises I had Karen work through:

- Settle into a quiet space and take three deep, slow breaths in and out through your nose.
- Focus in on where you're feeling pressure to act a certain way in your life and begin to curiously explore why.
- Start to listen to your thoughts and list out all the "shoulds" going through your head. Let it all out and set aside the judgment.

Through breath work and visualization exercises, we were able to shift her internal landscape to rely on her heart and intuition while letting go of her past guilt and sense of duty.

If you find yourself struggling with a bad case of the shoulds, here are a few tips on how to ditch the shoulds and rely more on your inner compass.

1. Ask yourself: Is the "should" I'm telling myself a true statement? If it's not, what is true?
2. Change your language. Instead of, "I should get a better job," say, "I want to get a better job." Do you recognize the difference between the two? The first one sounds forced, and the second sounds like a choice.
3. Ask yourself who or what is the source of this "should" statement. Does it come from your friends, family, or society? What is the intention of the "should"? To keep you safe? Often the "shoulds" start as good ideas or intentions but they simply don't serve us.
4. Lastly, ask yourself if these "shoulds" are helpful for you in your life. Do they create joy? What could you do differently?

Healing from burnout requires so much more than listening to our head and activating our logical brain (i.e., thinking our way out of burnout). We can learn how to tap into our whole self by activating our body, heart, and mind to join us on the journey toward living an extraordinary life.

As we align both our head and heart and choose to abandon the "shoulds" that no longer serve us, we may feel a little lost. We will need to discover what we truly believe in and what we want outside of our current superimposed societal restrictions. In the next chapter, we will begin to unravel these bound-up intricacies. You will begin to start thinking for yourself and discover who you truly are and want to be.

CHAPTER 5

IDENTITY—WHO ARE YOU?

During one of my *Hello, Head, Meet Heart* interviews, I held space for a woman who was transitioning into retirement and struggling with settling into her new identity—one without a corporate title. "I don't know who I am anymore," she said.

As our session ended, I thought back to one of the first times I heard the question asked: "Who are you?" It was the caterpillar in *Alice in Wonderland* asking Alice the question. Alice responded, "I don't know. I remember who I was when I woke up this morning, but I think I've changed a great deal since then" (Carroll 1866). This is so true.

As we evolve in life, this question bubbles up. Many individuals struggle to answer it. Why? Because as Alice summarized:

Life gets in the way. Somewhere along our hectic, messy, devastating, exhilarating lives, we forget to ask ourselves: "Does this decision align with who I am at my core? Does this fit the new me? What do I want?" We focus instead on the external forces in our lives like work and neglect the internal ones.

A big moment or transition in our life can force us to confront this question head on, most commonly when one chapter in our life closes and another chapter begins.

CLOSING THE CHAPTER

Haley worked at HP for thirty-six years in a variety of roles. She became one of the first women at HP to be in a senior vice president leadership position. Then the company decided to reorganize, and they began to decentralize the department. Her role expanded to the point she couldn't take it anymore, and she decided it was a good time to leave.

As Haley prepared to leave her job, she found herself in a stage of grief and struggled with staying in the anger phase about having to leave her career after thirty-six years. The anger got so bad she sought the counsel of a psychiatrist, who said to her, "Pretend it's three years from now. How do you want people to remember you? Do you want them to see you as an angry and disgruntled employee leaving or for what you accomplished while you were here?" This question immediately shifted her lens. She wanted to have a positive and lasting legacy, so she decided to let her anger go.

When Haley retired, she found she was unprepared for it. She thought she had planned for retirement for her entire career. She knew how much money she and her husband needed to save as they had met with their financial advisor and attended seminars. But she had not prepared for the emotional effects of retirement.

"Everyone prepares you for the financial impacts of retirement, but no one tells you you're going to lose your identity or suddenly your opinion won't count anymore. This can be extremely devastating to your soul. I wished I could have started exploring life outside of work more before actual retirement. I would have loved to have someone share their experience of retiring with me and walk me through the emotional stages of retirement."

CREATING A NEW CHAPTER/ROUTINE

As Haley and I talked about how to move through the stages of transition, and in her case retirement, she focused her energies on looking forward. She started creating some new routines she could try, which would be a comfortable fit for her. One of her biggest fears was she would be bored, end up watching the news all day, or take too many naps. She was cognizant of the fear when creating her plan. "I didn't want to be like several of my friends who just sat around and watched the news all day long. I wanted my life to still matter." Haley found an organization where she enjoyed working part-time and started to learn pickleball. The goal was to keep her mind and body moving and stay engaged.

WHEN WHO YOU ARE DOESN'T FIT

Throughout our life, some moments cause us to look at our identity, but we also face situations when who we think we are just doesn't fit with who we truly are. We feel misaligned.

As I was writing *Hello, Head, Meet Heart* one of my previous work colleagues—formerly known as Kim— shared with me that she had decided to transition to a man. Kim is now Finn. As I interviewed Finn, I asked him when he first asked himself the question: *Who am I?*

Finn explained he was raised in a super-conservative religious home. Growing up he hung out with his brothers mostly, but if he had to play with his sisters, he would build condos for their doll houses on the bookshelves. He hated playing with the dolls.

He described being uncomfortable in his own body. "Every time I looked in the mirror, I hated what I saw. I was like: Who is that person? That's not me. That's not what I feel like on the inside."

Throughout his childhood and into his adulthood Finn struggled with the internal battle raging inside him. Each time he dressed in feminine clothing or was identified as a female, it started bothering him more and more.

When Finn was in his fifties, he decided to officially transition from a woman to a man. At the time he was in a seventeen-year relationship with a female as a gay female. Once Finn shared his gender transition plan with his partner, she was supportive at first but later became distant and resentful as she felt she had been betrayed and lied to for so long.

"She felt like I had lied to her for seventeen years, but I tried to explain I did not lie to her. I could not tell her something I didn't fully understand. I was numb to who I truly was." Finn struggled with the realization he had also lied to himself for so long. His partner and he no longer speak, which was a huge loss to both of them. Finn describes this loss as being one of the hardest lessons he learned in choosing to walk away from his former life in order to save himself.

Finn is not alone in his struggles with identity. According to a recent article in Williams Institute, "How Many Adults and Youth Identify as Transgender in the United States?" the transgender population represents about 0.3 percent of American adults. This is a fairly large population. But how many transgender men and women decide to formally make the medical transition to another gender? The 2011 National Transgender Discrimination Survey found that 61 percent of trans and gender nonconforming respondents reported having medically transitioned, and 33 percent said they had surgically transitioned. About 14 percent of trans women and 72 percent of trans men said they don't ever want full reconstruction surgery (Herman 2022).

So, with such a big population at large and transgender people facing such a huge identity crisis, why are transgender adults not choosing to have the surgery? According to a recent interview on ABC with Dr. Norman Spack, she stated: "Being transgender is not about physical changes. It is about gender identity. For a transgender person, their gender identity does not align with their biological sex. For transgender people, their bodies below the brain do not define their gender status."

Since Finn's gender reassignment surgery, he says it's been a challenge for him to create a new life for himself in both his internal and external world.

Internally Finn said he feels more aligned with himself. He now recognizes the energy he spent hating what he saw every day in the mirror affected how he felt on the inside. When the dysphoria started to lessen, his external self started to fit more like what he felt inside. Those two came together. His head and heart aligned.

When asking him how he feels about reconciling the *his* and *her* pieces of himself, he said this: "After I had the official surgery, I've become much more comfortable with the feminine parts of me. And I treasure the sensitive part, the feminine energy I felt so uncomfortable with before. Now that my body aligns with everything else, I have become comfortable. I'm grateful for my experience as a woman. I believe having been a woman makes me a better man."

In the external world, Finn describes his transition as being a very lonely time: "I'm still part of the queer community, but there's very much this strong rejection from the lesbian community. My appearance is vastly different. I've found it to be a real struggle to find where I fit in. I don't fit with the macho guys. The group I'm most comfortable with is women, but I can tell it's making them uncomfortable. It's like why is this guy hanging around?"

Often Finn spends time alone and outside. He has learned to be patient making connections built around acceptance, kindness, and trust. He has managed to make a few friends, mostly people who have experienced burnout, lost their identity, and have gone through deaths and loss.

When I asked Finn how he could live in misery for so long, his response was one of true honesty: "I think I covered it up with busyness. I gave myself and my time away more than I should have to work. I would never again work fifty to sixty hours a week because it kept me from aligning with myself. It caused me problems in my relationship, to put my friendships second, and it caused me to put myself even further down on the list. I wasn't listening to myself. I wasn't creating downtime or quiet time. I wasn't taking space to really get in tune with myself and just listen. I would be too exhausted. I would just rest. The difference between recovery and trying to build back energy and restore yourself is different than having a peaceful time when you're already rested and able to tune into yourself."

Hearing Finn's story about the importance of listening to the voice inside you, which gets louder and louder as time evolves, reminds us you cannot truly live a life worth living unless you know and accept who you truly are. Only when you are in the moments of peace can you be honest with yourself and work toward assembling all the pieces of you so you can become whole.

ASSEMBLING YOUR PUZZLE

If you are struggling with knowing who you are, here is an exercise you can try to begin to discover the answer.

Start with what you know. Grab a piece of paper and a pen. On the top of the page write: "Who I am and What I love." You are going to craft a personal mosaic. Think about all facets of you: who you are at work, at home, and in your community. Example: "I am adventurous. I love to explore." Write down as many things as you can. Exhaust the list.

Eliminate. Reflect on the "should" in your life. Make a list of things you are compromising on that do not align with your mosaic. Try to eliminate as many of the "shoulds" as you can.

Explore. Often we feel lost because we are bored with our lives. We have stopped exploring. Take an hour each week to explore one of the statements you wrote in your mosaic. If you wrote: "I am adventurous," but you are watching TV every night, research a rock gym, dance class, or outdoor club you could join.

As you complete these exercises and begin to get clearer about who you are, it is normal if fear starts to creep into you. It is important to pause and acknowledge assembling your puzzle isn't easy. It takes work, and growth isn't circular. It is a spiral. Who you are today won't be the same *you* next year or even in ten years. Your puzzle will need to be assembled and reassembled. It might always feel scary.

When you focus on behaviors and activities that truly align with what you want and eliminate the busyness, the external noise, and the "shoulds," you will discover the answer to who you are has been inside you all along. In the next chapter, we will tackle how to address your fear head-on and get to a more secure place to access joy in your life.

CHAPTER 6

CONVERSATIONS WITH FEAR

———

"Focus on where you want to go, not on what you fear."

—TONY ROBBINS

A daily question I continued to ponder—one that kept me up at night—was how in the hell was I going to figure out what I wanted to do with my life when I didn't even know where to begin?

During my stay at the retreat center in Arizona, I met with a spiritual guidance counselor who changed my life. Her name was Theresa. The purpose of the session was for me to gain clarity. During our first session, Theresa suggested I start with three principles: mission, mantra, and mindfulness.

I rolled my eyes. Yeah, it sounded good, but I told her I needed some substance. She started laughing. She explained the importance of reframing clarity in my mind. Instead of me looking at the "What am I going to do next?" question from a cerebral standpoint—a logical and business way as I always have—I should try instead to look at it from a heart perspective.

I snorted. "You cannot feel your way into a new life. You have to think about the consequences, decide how you are going to make money, and analyze the risks." I could already feel my anxiety creeping into the room.

Theresa kindly smiled and paused, "If you want to live a life full of joy and meaning, you cannot ask what the world needs. Ask yourself instead what makes you come alive because the world needs people who come alive."

Wow! This statement reverberated to my core. I was looking at this all wrong. I never considered choosing a path that brought me joy. I bet I couldn't even list three things that brought me joy. I hadn't felt true joy in at least a year.

Theresa asked me to begin with an exercise: "What I'm going to ask you to do is pick a blank page in your journal and draw a line down the middle of the page. Next, I am going to ask you to list on the left side what brings you joy."

Oh, Jesus here we go. Just what I just said I couldn't do. I took a deep breath and began quickly jotting down my task.

Here was my list: Peter (my husband), Palmer (my dog), my patients (from my previous job in healthcare), close friends, and my mom and dad.

"Okay, I'm done," I said after three minutes.

"Can you share your list with me?" she asked.

"Sure," I said and read her my list.

She became very quiet. "Hannah, is there anything just for you on here?"

"Yes, Peter and Palmer I guess."

"Can you expand a little more and write down an activity or description when you felt joy?"

"Sure," I said.

I closed my eyes and took a breath. As my lungs expanded with air, so did my list. The words came quickly onto the page: sun, being next to water, nature, playing with my dog, decorating, writing, reading, taking a bath, traveling, eating good food, feeling cozy in my pajamas, cuddling with my husband. I looked up at her from the new list. Wow, this list felt different.

She smiled at me. "I wish you could have seen your face during both exercises. In the first one, you were head down, hard focused on completing your assignment. The second time, you were smiling, your posture changed, and I felt your joy. That is the difference between leaning into your heart instead of your head."

The patterns of the last twenty years of my life became so clear. Not only had I become hardened to survive in my career, I had chosen to turn away from joy. I had turned toward work and immersed myself in task-oriented busyness like the limitless emails and the pressure of always being on and available to my staff, peers, and management.

I was known as a go-to person at work. People needed me and I delivered. But I had also turned away from myself. I had ignored the signs of my distress: a high blood pressure diagnosis, panic attacks, a diagnosis of fatty liver disease, insomnia, and finally depression, which led me down a dark, dark path contemplating ending it all.

My default was to simply "busy" myself, to never stop going or moving instead toward the direction I thought I *should* be going. My body screamed *caution, stop, slippery conditions ahead,* but I kept my foot on the gas and said, *Fuck you,* to myself. This reflection rocked me to the core. Why did this happen and how could I have done this to myself? The answer I could come up with—*fear.* I was afraid to address what would come up for me if I slowed down. I was afraid of the answers.

HELLO, FEAR
"So how do I move through the fear to get to the joy?" I asked Theresa.

As we talked through this question, Theresa shared with me a tactic for addressing my fear as it comes. Have you heard the premise from Thich Nhat Hanh? You say to the fear feeling as it comes: "Hello, my little fear, I see you, and I am going to take care of you today."

The concept is as you see the fear coming, you address it head-on and you don't let your fear drive you. Instead, think of your life as a car. You are the driver, and the fear is your passenger. I loved this concept. I was an excellent driver, a fast one too. The concept was also a visual one I could picture. If I was afraid of failing, and I said to the fear, "I see you, but I am going to try XYZ anyway," the fear became powerless and obsolete.

Theresa also explained being in a constant state of fear signals to us we need to turn toward ourselves more as too many external forces are at play. The focus of listening to yourself, identifying what you need, and saying to yourself, *I am here for you,* helps you to shift from an external focus to an internal one. This will keep you on the right track to avoid abandoning your younger self—your true inner diamond.

In a way, it was almost like I was saving someone else and not myself because of my being an empath and a fixer. It was easy to think about just fixing someone else, a.k.a. my avatar of Hannah versus me. I could justify the avatar needed help, but the reality was the woman was me.

So, I began a project with a small plan. Every day I was going to do something for myself that focused on the components of body, mind, and spirit. Body—moving my body, working out, taking the dog for a walk. Mind—reading a new article on something new or listening to a podcast. Spirit—laughing more, loving, cuddling, and more resting.

During this period, I would often wake up at three o'clock in the morning and think about what I was doing walking away from such a big career. The panic would come on, and then I would just gently remind myself again that nothing could be worse than losing who you are or putting your health at risk.

Everyone making a big transformation has to have important conversations with themselves as well as with others—conversations with fear, conversations with hope, and conversations that break apart everything you thought you knew about yourself. The biggest thing holding us back from having these conversations is *fear*. We are scared of how our loved ones will react to us sharing out loud with them what we have been saying to ourselves inside for so long.

I'll be honest. I struggled with this and the sequencing of it. How much should I tell? When should I tell it? I searched online for resources I could use to begin even starting to have the conversation. Feeling dissatisfied with my search, I created my prompts and used them to guide my conversations with myself, my husband, family, and friends.

As I talked with more and more people, I found I wasn't alone in my fears.

My friend Maggie struggled with the fear of being judged by her family when wanting to share a pivotal point in her life. When she decided to take a big leap to quit her job, buy a sailboat, and become a travel writer, she became fearful of how her parents and family would react to the decision. She didn't know how to tell them or what to say. She wanted their support and for them to come along on the exciting ride, but once she told them of her plans, she found it was a lot for them to mentally grasp, and they tried to convince her she needed to keep her day job and accept the monotony of her old life. She was glad she shared the news with her family, but it saddened her they couldn't get past their preconceived fears for her.

As you hear these stories, do any of them resonate with you? Are you afraid to share what's going on with you? Are you worried you will be judged? Are you worried about having a difference of opinion from someone you love? Are you worried no one will support you? Are you afraid of failing? Are you scared of what's next? Are you scared of stepping outside your comfort zone? These fears surface for so many of us, and they are all real. The problem is most people cling to their fears because they believe they're a part of who they are.

Before you can begin to address the fear, you have to be aware your fears are causing strain in your life. It's easy to get so attached to your thoughts and feelings you think they are all that exists, but this isn't true. You are not your fears. You are the awareness experiencing it.

Here are a few things for you to work through:

Identify: Get specific about what exactly you are afraid of. Pay attention to the images in your head about the situation.

What is happening in them? What are you scared of? Describe what is happening.

Curious: Get curious about what thoughts generate your fear. Where do you feel the fear? How do you react to it? What color does it have?

Bring your fear to the present: What are you lacking right now? Tapping into the now can be as simple as feeling your body and breathing. *The Power of Now* by Eckhart Tolle is a great book to refer to.

Overcoming fear is a learned skill, and it takes time. Don't rush yourself. By paying attention to *what, how,* and *where* the fear is coming from, you can understand the fear is not a part of *who* you are. It is designed to keep us safe but not to drive our choices and actions.

Once you gain more skills in overcoming some of your fears, you can begin to share your internal world with your external world.

You will want to be mindful of choosing the right time and right place to have these conversations. I would suggest you schedule a time in advance and also check in with your partner's emotions before beginning to talk about any of these things. Once you have a time and place and have checked in with your partner, use these prompts as a guide to help you talk through your internal dialogue with friends, family, and support system in your life:

- Describe what you've been experiencing during this time of transition. Share how it's been for you—emotionally, physically, etc. Be as specific as you can within your comfort zone.
- Tell them what options you've been exploring and what you've learned about yourself.
- What new ways of thinking have you developed?
- Ask them what they've noticed about you during this time. Invite them to offer their suggestions and perspectives about a transition they have been through.
- Share what support you may need from them, if any. Be as specific as you can within your comfort zone.

This has been a wonderful tool for many of my clients to use when they have struggled with speaking with their partners and family members about a life transition they have faced.

My client Catherine used these prompts as a guide when she was struggling with losing her identity as a retiree. Her husband was still working, and she had recently retired. Catherine wanted to speak with Jim about how she was feeling, but she didn't know how to start the conversation. She was worried she would get caught up in the emotion of how she was feeling and fail to communicate what she needed from him.

"I wanted to talk with Jim about how I was feeling since I retired. We had been planning this transition for years, but once I retired, I realized I missed working with students. I was struggling with where to start to share all the things that had been swirling around in my mind. The prompts you provided were helpful for me to use as a guide to begin the conversation."

By taking the time to organize your thoughts and words using the prompts above, you can practice having these conversations in a safe space until you become more comfortable sharing with your larger community.

As these conversations occur, you may find yourself wondering how much information you should share. You aren't alone. Many of my clients have worried about sharing too much or too little. In the next chapter, we will highlight the importance of overcoming these tough conversations, being vulnerable with others, and learning to lean into forgiveness for yourself and others.

CHAPTER 7

MISTAKES AND FORGIVENESS

"To forgive is to set a prisoner free and realize the prisoner was you."

—LEWIS B. SMEDES

One of the main causes of my burnout was feeling like I had to be perfect all the time. I was afraid of making mistakes, and I was afraid of the shame that came along with making them.

As I moved along in my burnout recovery journey, I had to redesign and create a new narrative around the importance and allowance of mistakes, and I had to form a new relationship with them. I found it challenging to switch gears from fear of failure to acceptance of failure. After so many years of paddling frantically below the surface and behind the scenes, my failure was in private. I didn't allow it to be in public. You could say I was the hardest on myself because of the way I was raised. And because of societal expectations, I was always supposed to be better, stronger, faster, and quicker. But in essence, the only real way I was able to succeed and exceed so much was because I failed quickly.

Being afraid to make mistakes affected my career in so many ways. I was in an industry and culture that had a lot of competition among women. I was guilty of judging several women I worked with when they made a mistake instead of supporting them. As I look back now, I am so angry and disappointed in myself for not reaching out to help them and instead silently standing by while they were sabotaged by others.

I contemplated whether to write this in the book because, in essence, I'm laying it all on the line. But the reality is I cannot ask you to be vulnerable unless I do the same. I need to leave it all on the page and share with you those defining moments in my life that contributed to my burnout.

As I've talked with hundreds of women over the last few months, their stories are similar. Many of them are ashamed of how they've treated other women in their life or stayed silent when they should have spoken up. It is a silent disease of judgment when women don't feel strong enough within themselves to be strong enough for someone else.

As I delved into this topic further, I became curious as to why, as women, we expect the most from ourselves and hold each other to these impossible standards as we are attempting to just survive. As I was writing this chapter, it just so happened, I was recording season 3 of the *She Burns with Hannah Austin* podcast. Season 3's topic was "Women Gamechangers." My guest for the day was Cindy Gallop, a woman who is a true game-changer in her industry. Cindy is the CEPO/Founder of MakeLoveNotPorn, the world's first and only user-generated, human-curated social sex video-sharing platform, which helps end rape culture by doing something very simple, showing you how wonderful great, consensual, communicative sex is in the real world. It role models good sexual values and behavior and makes it all aspirational versus what you see in porn and popular culture.

During our discussion, I asked Cindy why she thought women were so afraid of making mistakes and why women were so competitive.

Cindy describes this problem as Highlander Syndrome. Although the real definition of Highlander Syndrome is a medical condition in which the body ages at a very slow or an almost negligible rate (Troup 2022), Cindy uses the term to describe when a member of a marginalized community (men), once having achieved some level of privilege becomes a gatekeeper to prevent other marginalized people from achieving the same privilege (women). Cindy summarized there can be only *one* in a male-dominated business world, in a male-dominated industry, which every industry is.

As women, we are taught at an early age there is only room for one token woman on the leadership team, board, or project. This forces women to compete with other women. It's the fault of patriarchal norms in a gender-unequal world. Cindy went on to say because of the unjust and unequal nature of this dilemma, the opportunity for us as women is to go against the grain of the system, reject the perfectionistic culture, and come together to remake the world to be the way we want it to be.

As I was speaking with my best friend Katie about this concept, I brought up the conversation of competition among women. "This reminds me of what happened with Naomi Campbell and Tyra Banks," she spoke. Although they were two of the most famous supermodels in history, Tyra Banks and Naomi Campbell were sworn enemies.

According to an exposé published in *The List* magazine, the trouble started when Banks shared that her idol, Campbell wasn't friendly to her when Banks was first starting out in the industry (Keogh 2021). As Katie and I discussed the toxicity of Tyra and Naomi's relationship, hearing this story was so relatable to instances in my life and my clients' lives. This example truly highlighted the scarcity mentality so many of us women face where we believe only ONE woman can be on top in a male-dominated world.

STEPPING OUTSIDE THE *ONE* MIND-SET

As my journey evolved, I wanted to learn *how* to give myself some grace around making mistakes. However, to do this, I needed to surround myself with people who fostered vulnerability and saw making mistakes as a good thing.

One of my biggest regrets overall was being ashamed of the mistakes I made and not allowing a community of peers, managers, and leaders to support me around making those mistakes. As I look back, I think about all the growth I missed out on by being silent and internalizing my shame and anger around those mistakes.

To keep moving forward, I knew I needed to step outside of the *one* mind-set. I began to take the steps needed to seek out other women who were open to being vulnerable and who were creating new and expansive ways to learn to accept themselves and be forgiving of themselves and others.

This was new territory for me. How was I going to find these women? At first, I found it humorous because at the age of forty-one I was on a journey to find some new friends, but as I started to brainstorm how I was going to find these women, it dawned on me: *What if I am searching for women who are also searching for someone like me?*

I set the goal for myself to join three networks: one group focused on my professional side, one to activate the physical, and one to nurture my spiritual and growth side. I chose the networking group Ellevate Network to meet the professional category. I joined classes at my local gym to satisfy the physical category. And to ignite my growth spiritually, I chose a book-writing group called Book Doulas. I found these contacts through my research on Google and by asking people on my close Facebook groups for recommendations.

By joining these three different arenas, I was placed in the company of women who wanted to grow and learn, emotionally and professionally. They reinforced me to be more vulnerable with my mistakes, learn *how* to ask for help, and hardwire habits and new skills to support other women in these networks.

As I look back at my journey, leaving the corporate environment and starting my own company allowed me to figure out what I stood for, who I wanted to surround myself with, and how I wanted to be as a leader. We always hear about a speak-up culture. We always hear about failing quickly and learning from it. But it's hard to fail quickly. It's hard to fail in public. It's painful. It's embarrassing. It's scary. To move forward, we need to create a safety net for ourselves to build new habits and processes in our day-to-day lives, reinforcing that making mistakes is welcome and necessary for growth.

Here is a routine I practice to help me create new habits and change my relationship and internal dialogue around making mistakes:

- When judgment starts to creep up on my mind, I put a hand on my heart and take a deep breath.
- I remind myself my value does not reside in the outcome or performance of the task I am judging myself on.
- I ask myself, *Did I do my best?*
- If I did, I acknowledge and tell myself: *Good job, Hannah, I'm proud of you.*
- If I am disappointed in myself, I ask myself: *What did I learn from this experience?*

- I say to myself, *Next time I will try XYZ, but I am proud of myself for putting myself out there and trying.*

MISTAKES ARE HEALTHY

As I started building new routines in my life, I shared some of my learnings with the new community of women I was building in my life. We traded stories about how we learned to normalize mistakes.

My peer Jenny shared she learned from her manager *how* to make and own a mistake. Seeing her manager have a healthy outlook on mistakes gave her permission to make a mistake.

"When my manager made a mistake, she said, 'Oops, I messed up.' Or, 'I forgot to send that to you. That's on me. Let me go fix it.' This ownership suddenly created a culture that spoke honestly about failure and reinforced it's okay to make a mistake. It's good to mess up and have the freedom to say, 'I messed up.' Her outlook and the example she set made me feel freer and only helped me and the other employees at the company."

As Jenny shared this story with me, I loved the idea that acknowledging your mistakes could lead you to feel freer. Lighter. I decided at that moment I liked how it sounded, and I was going to adopt this approach as I built my company and mentored others.

My colleague Martha, who was a competitive gymnast, grew up in a competitive environment. At the beginning of her career, she struggled with constantly comparing herself to her other female teammates and competitors. The sport in itself led to this competitive nature. Because she started as a gymnast at an early age, she struggled with issues around self-identity, bulimia, and body dysmorphia.

She would wake up every day and beat herself up over a mistake at practice or when she fell off of the beam. Her obsession with competing and making mistakes became so toxic she became burned out and quit competing. After receiving help for years in therapy, she found ways to overcome her fear of failure. "As I've gotten more in tune with myself and who I am, I am not afraid to fail."

Martha learned to address her mistakes and failures head-on. She created a balance between healthy competition and mistakes, learning after so many years of being hard on herself to forgive. She stated, "When I see new gymnasts or athletes now, I make a point to share that mistakes are healthy. I praise them for the effort and energy they put into their routines instead of focusing on the result."

As you start to strengthen your "mistake muscles," you might find you will continue to make some old mistakes repeatedly. An example of this may be how you treated someone, an action you took that hurt yourself, or a lesson you continue to learn time and time again yet can't seem to master. Whatever it is, acknowledging you aren't going to always make the right decision, say the right thing, or do the right is important. Life is messy, not perfect, and mistakes are about learning.

Take a moment and reflect on some of the mistakes you've made and how you've dealt with them.

REFLECTION

What comes up for you when you think about your relationship with mistakes? Here are some questions for you to reflect on and answer:

- How do you feel when you make a mistake?
- When you make a mistake, who do you tell?
- How do you acknowledge that you made the mistake?
- What have you learned from your mistakes?
- Do you look at mistakes as a part of your life process or do you look at them with regret?

FORGIVENESS

After you completed the reflection exercise, did any regret show up for you? If so, what do you need to do to forgive yourself and move forward? Do you need to apologize to someone? Perhaps you want to write yourself a letter and burn it. Maybe you want to create an action or learning plan about what you might do differently in the future if a similar situation comes up for you. Whatever will help you to move through the mistake, do it. If you don't know how to move through it, call me. It is important to forgive yourself and honor yourself in the growth you've made from the mistake.

Here are some actionable strategies you can adopt for future situations:

- When a similar XYZ situation arises in the future, I will:
  - Ask for more information to clarify the situation before I act.

- Place my hand on my heart, breathe deeply and feel the emotion that comes up for me.
- Acknowledge the shame that bubbles up post-mistake, be kind to me, and let it go.

These are all actionable strategies my clients and colleagues have found to be helpful. However, at times we simply can't forget some mistakes.

One pattern of mistakes kept haunting me as I did this exercise. The competition I have acted on against my women peers has been one of the biggest wounds of my life. I have learned to forgive myself for those actions and inactions. Every day as the CEO of a woman-empowerment company, I actively seek out ways I can support other women in business, and through the building of each relationship, I feel the wound is healing a little bit more.

It is important to note that making mistakes isn't a bad thing, and not every mistake comes with regret. Mistakes are normal, and in fact, they are a part of life—a part of learning and growing. Without mistakes, there is no growth.

In the next chapter, we will explore what happens after you've acknowledged the impact mistakes have had in your life, and you've given yourself the gift of forgiveness but are experiencing a setback. I will show you how you can share the lessons you've learned from setbacks and mistake-mapping to shift your focus to the blessings that lie ahead.

CHAPTER 8

SETBACKS AND BLESSINGS

"Every setback is an invitation to grow. To evolve and come back better."

—SHEENA JAYNE MARTIN

In May 2022, halfway through writing this book, I had a major setback. I had just finished writing my first draft manuscript, and I got incredible news. I was given the green light from my editing and publishing team. To put this milestone in perspective, only 2 percent of authors get a green light to move forward in the book writing process. Getting the green light was an acknowledgment this book would be coming to life, an acknowledgment you would be reading these pages. It had been a dream of mine for decades and now the dream was coming true. I would like to say this setback was just a little bit of writer's block, but the reality was I stumbled back into my old emotional numbing patterns. I was feeling unworthy and was choosing to fill the void of unworthiness with food. Lots of it.

WHAT IS EMOTIONAL NUMBING?

"Emotional numbing happens when we keep ourselves busy with work, self-medicate with alcohol or drugs, or seek pleasure in unhealthy habits. Often these behaviors run in a repeating cycle. We binge eat or drink, clean up our act, dive into an impossible to-do list, get overwhelmed, and repeat" (Michael 2020).

My emotional numbing first started in college. I had been away from home for the first time, and although I had a busy social life in the outside world, I was lonely inside. When I began to feel lonely, I would go to the dining hall to fill my loneliness. When I was scared, I would eat in my dorm room. It wasn't until my sophomore year in college during a session with my therapist in my hometown that I was honest with her about how ashamed I was of what I was doing. She described it as emotional numbing. For the past twenty years, my weight has fluctuated because of this.

The good news is now, twenty years later as I began to learn to tap into living a conscious life, I had become more aware of what emotional numbing was and those patterns and triggers when they started to bubble up for me. It just so happened during this week when I was having my setback, I had a client who was also struggling with a setback of her own.

They say the universe only puts those experiences in your life you need to learn, or in my case re-learn, and it couldn't have been truer at this moment.

UNWORTHINESS AND WINE

My client Renee came to me by way of a referral. I helped one of her colleagues through her burnout recovery journey. During our first session together, Renee described that she had been passed up for a promotion at work, and she was stuck in the vicious cycle of self-hatred, feeling unworthy and unfulfilled. She would go home in the evenings, order food through GrubHub or Uber Eats, and pick out a bottle of wine. She would eat the salt-ridden take-out food and drink the wine while standing at her kitchen counter watching Netflix. This was her routine every night. She would often finish the entire bottle by herself and then wake up in the morning, tired, thirsty, ashamed, and hungover. The self-hatred and guilt would creep in, and it would be a vicious weekly cycle.

During our sessions, we talked a lot about why she chose alcohol as her escape, and she told me she used to be an athlete. The adrenaline and buzz she would feel after a race or working out was a similar feeling to what she would get initially when she started drinking alcohol. She would feel lighter, high, on top of the world.

She forgot about work, her perceived failures, and the life she wanted to live but wasn't living. I asked her why she stopped working out, and she said she had an injury she hadn't been able to heal from. Since then, she had chosen to use alcohol as a replacement.

Renee shared how she felt about herself, and we started the process of rewiring her thought patterns, slowly unraveling her disappointments, making a plan for her at work, and setting a clear outcome-oriented goal for her to prioritize her health and healing from her injury once and for all.

To have Renee start the process of rewiring her thought patterns, I asked her to construct a visual pride board she could hang on the wall in her office and see every day. On one side of the board, I asked her to list all of the accomplishments she was proud of in her work life, and on the other side of the board, I asked her to write down her learnings from the disappointments—not the disappointments themselves.

This board was the place she was to refer to when she started to feel unworthy or if she started to go down the self-hatred road. Next, I asked her to set one to two work goals and place them on the bottom of the board. From there we used the key learnings from her past disappointments to create a plan for her to accomplish her set goals.

For example, one of her work goals was to be promoted to a senior director job. Since she had been passed up for promotion, she had started to be cynical and negative during meetings because of her disappointment. She had expressed she didn't want to be this way. She was just hurt.

We decided to craft an expected behavior plan for her with the goal in mind for her to compliment a colleague consciously and proactively or actively participate in a positive conversation at work. This, in turn, would reinforce a new habit and create a positive atmosphere for both Renee and her team. After a few weeks, Renee began to feel more positive and less isolated by her team, and she was asked to be on the summer league kickball team.

Through more engagement sessions, she began to cut back on alcohol and her body began to heal with getting regular exercise. Renee now has a new role and is feeling better about who she is and what she is worth, and she's getting stronger physically every day.

Renee and I are not alone. So many women have these silent vices, whether it's food, sex, or alcohol, no matter what it is— all of these chosen avenues are used for the same purpose—to attempt to close the wound within us. However, it has the opposite effect. It leaves the wound red and raw, preventing us from healing.

NUMBING THE DEEP WOUNDS WITHIN US

Food and alcohol aren't the only things people turn to in order to give themselves bodily sensations while numbing out. My client Carly used affection and sex as her outlet to numb herself due to her history of sexual abuse. If she was in a dark place in her life, she would go on Tinder or a dating app, meet up with a guy and sleep with him.

This would temporarily relieve her feelings and emotions and ultimately numb her. But then the next morning or the next day she would be filled with a healthy self-hatred. This was a vicious cycle because it left her feeling depleted, used, and unworthy. As Carly and I unpacked her journey, it was never about the physical piece for her. It was about trying to feel something. She was desperately trying to feel loved and in control. She knew deep down she was lying to herself, but she kept doing it because she wanted so badly to feel love, feel safe, and feel something good for a change.

My clients and colleagues are intelligent people. They know what they're doing isn't working, but they don't know how else to stop the pain until the inconvenience of the toxic cyclical life manifests itself through a diagnosis of diabetes, excessive weight gain, a traumatic sexual experience, or burnout. Often these situations arise before you realize these behaviors are not serving you. They never have.

With my recent setback, I knew numbing myself with food wouldn't work due to experience. I knew it would provide some immediate relief, even though the shame and disgust would come after the relief. But this time after I had stuffed my face with takeout sushi, I looked at all of the cartons around me and I just felt sad for myself. I began to speak to myself, "You are scared. This is a scary step in your life. You used to need this behavior to calm down, but now you don't."

At that moment, the voice of feeding the monster began to get quieter than my compassion for myself. I silenced the monster and recognized I needed to have some self-compassion and acceptance and stop blaming myself for my setback.

TURNING TOWARD THE EXTERNAL
Attempting to numb and escape our internal lack of control, self-hatred, failures, fears, grief, and disappointments are only a few reasons we turn to external forces such as food,

sex, alcohol, and work. Other reasons could include mental or emotional abuse, PTSD, overwhelming stress, and substance misuse. No matter what your reason is, by turning toward the external and away from yourself, you deepen the wound inside you.

A common setback for many of us is the notion of being scared to succeed. I have had times in my life where things have started going well for me, or they became too easy, and then I quit the task because it became too scary or more real. As women we can create obstacles, so we don't complete things because we are scared to get what we want. We dumb ourselves down. We become less than. We may think if it's not hard, it's not worth it to us. If it's too easy, we don't trust it. We say to ourselves, "It's too good to be true." It's a merry-go-round of fear, and it's terrifying.

So, what is the answer to getting off of these toxic merry-go-rounds once and for all? I call it the SAUS method:

- S—Stop. Breathe, take a slow deep breath, and place your hand on your heart.
- A—Acknowledge your feelings. Use an "I am" or an "I did" statement.
- U—Unpack your emotions. Use an "I feel" statement.
- S—Shift your energy.

It is important to know as painful as feeling the feelings can be for us, we have feelings for a reason. By stopping and acknowledging those feelings, we can use them as clues to know what our feelings are telling us. We can gather extremely helpful information there.

By replacing our numbing habits with healthier activities, we can feel the feelings in a safe and restorative manner.

Here are a few activities you can shift your energy to:

- Learn to take walks.
- Involve yourself with a project.
- Have a regular coffee or lunch date with a friend.
- Create a "feelings" journal. Draw or write down what you're feeling so you can see it in black and white.

By acknowledging and addressing your numbness head-on, you are taking a big and brave step. As you begin to shift your energy toward these new activities, you will begin to feel yourself soften and lighten. You will realize happiness and joy wouldn't exist without counter emotions like sadness, fear, pain, and anger. You will begin to take back control of your own life and stop the merry-go-round. You will forever be changed.

As we explore the next chapter, we will dive into what happens when you get stuck in only one side of your brain and begin second-guessing yourself. I will show you how to activate and align your whole self to move steadily forward on your journey.

CHAPTER 9

SECOND GUESSING

"Your ego is your soul's worst enemy."

—*RUSTY ERIC*

What no one tells you about the process of quitting your job to find your inner joy and passion is that it can be a painful, identity-stripping, raw, and tireless journey. My advice is not to do it right away as you will need faith in yourself and a strong support system. I was fortunate I had both, but the reality is life goes on, your old coworkers start to reach out less, and your previous company moves on without you. You are replaceable. You will be remembered but quickly forgotten. This was a painful lesson for me to learn.

However, the most painful of all the lessons was that my entire self-worth and identity were wrapped up and nicely packaged as a "career." As a forty-one-year-old childless woman, I could only point to one thing being my lasting life legacy—my career, which I no longer had. At the retreat center, I learned I needed to delve into how I got to the place I was at this moment. I needed to examine how I had become so depleted. During my spiritual guidance session, my guru Theresa shared some key concepts and insights with me.

She explained you have two selves—your unique self and your enduring self. The unique or (small self) is described as what makes you, you. This includes your traits, history, personality, and values. The enduring or (big self) is described as your inner diamond. This is your healing ground within yourself.

As I unpacked these concepts, I discovered when I chose to leave my job, I left my false sense of self in that role. In essence, I abandoned and excavated the layers around me that were preventing me from growing. I felt stuck in my situation because I was used to certain patterns of behavior. Because they were useful to me in the past, the patterns became more harmful than useful as I continued to apply an old formula to the new space I wanted for my life.

THE SELVES

Unpacking the concept of "the self" was a pivotal point in my burnout recovery. Because it was such a powerful ah-ha in my journey, I wanted to share it with my clients to apply it to their lives. As I began to research the theory more, I found the concept of the true and false self has been a long-existing concept in philosophy. The true self (also known as the real self, authentic self, original self, and vulnerable self) and false self (also known as fake self, idealized self, superficial self, and pseudo self) are psychological concepts, originally introduced into psychoanalysis in 1960 by Donald Winnicott (Burkhardt 2020).

During my research, I came across an alternative concept: The "Three Face Theory." Dubbed a Japanese proverb, the Three Face theory says we, as humans, have three faces, each presented to a different category of people. The first face is what we show to the world—diplomatic and perfect. The second face is the one we show to our family and friends—semi-real but not the truest. Lastly, the third face is the one we hide from everyone. We never show this to anyone, yet it's often the truest reflection of who we are (Kazmi 2021).

Both concepts highlighted the need for additional exploration to aid in the quest to limit second-guessing yourself.

THE FALSE SELF

In his article "You Are Not What You Think You Are—the False Self, the Ego, and the True Self," Michael Burkhardt quotes English psychoanalyst and child psychologist Donald Winnicott as saying: "The false self is an artificial persona people create very early in life to protect themselves from re-experiencing developmental trauma, shock, and stress in close relationships."

THE TRUE SELF

According to Burkhardt, the true self has two perspectives: a psychological one and a spiritual perspective. He states if you are on a quest to tap into your true self, the quest itself will create discomfort before giving you a new sense of freedom. It will involve uncovering your delusionary thoughts. You will need to dive deep into your unsolved sides, insecurities, and fears as well as your strengths. But it will be worth it, and as a result, you'll connect back to your inner voice, which knows and always has known what is best for you and the people around you.

My past formula was the belief (and false self-recipe) that I was only of value when I was able to produce or create something. In essence, I had to always earn my worth. I earned my worth by working hard and being and doing good. A great reflection on this came from Brené Brown who said: "You either walk inside your story and own it or you stand outside your story and hustle for your worthiness."

Brown believes our worthiness lives inside our stories. We have a choice to own those stories and share them with people who have earned the right to hear them, or we can spend our time hustling for our worthiness, constantly proving, perfecting, performing, and pleasing on a never-ending search for satisfaction. My burnout was a big wake-up call, showing me I was tired of hustling for my worthiness, and I was now ready to walk into my own story.

I stood outside my story and in my false self for so many years by adhering to norms, others' approval, wealth, and social status. I labeled myself as being a good person if I took care of everyone else first and then checked in on myself last. I always joked with my team at work that I needed to check in on "my chickens" before "mama hen" could relax. I was so focused on external activities I abandoned my true self in the process. I was yearning to find my true self beneath the exterior of a title. My true self was kind, fun, energetic, and playful—not controlling and directive.

Making the pivot from standing outside of my story to walking inside was challenging along the way. As I started down the road of unraveling who I was without my career and former life, I struggled with second-guessing myself in a variety of ways. It started with: "Why can't I be happy in my job? I have a job most people would dream of."

Then I began to second-guess whether or not I should leave. And then after I left, I began to second-guess whether or not I made a huge mistake in leaving. The second-guessing left me stuck and paralyzed, hindering me from moving forward.

In my quest for why I was second-guessing myself, I found I was not alone. According to author Agapi Stassinopoulos, "We stay stuck because we think, *Well, maybe I should do this,* or, *I don't know how to do it,* and we start to give our authority over to our other voices which are depleting us. So, we stay stuck in a place that doesn't work for us, and we feel depleted because there's a feeling of not trusting ourselves. The problem is we think we have to have it all figured out, and we're forgetting the fact life doesn't come with a user's manual—we have to just make it up as we go along." To expand on this argument Stassinopoulos quoted Louis C.K.: "Feeling unsure and lost is part of your path. Don't avoid it. See what those feelings are showing you and use it. Take a breath. You'll be okay, even if you don't feel okay all the time."

It was helpful to know I wasn't alone in my thoughts, but as the second-guessing continued, I knew I needed more help with some coping strategies on how to stop second-guessing myself. I reached out to Mariah, my therapist, for support. During our sessions, she shared with me the concept of the Inner Critic.

SO, WHAT IS MY INNER CRITIC?

According to a recent article by Walsh in *Good Therapy*, our inner critic refers to an inner voice that judges, criticizes, or demeans a person whether or not self-criticism is objectively justified. A highly active inner critic can take a toll on one's emotional well-being and self-esteem.

ADDRESSING THE INNER CRITIC

So how do we stop second-guessing ourselves and address those annoying negative voices in our heads—our "inner critics"? They do not respond well to us silencing them. Instead, they keep coming back, asking for more attention. Your inner critic wants to be heard, and if you're ever going to create healthy, anti-burnout boundaries, you'll have to hear them out. Before you listen too closely, though, you need to get to know them a little better because let's be honest. You wouldn't take such personal advice from just anyone.

The first step is to define your inner critic. Imagine them as an imaginary character in the room, like an annoying little sister or brother. The premise is, if your inner critic is allowed to be "in the room" and made to feel heard, they won't need to shout to be heard, and eventually, the noise will stop all together. Then, once you have a clear picture of who your critic is, you'll be able to set boundaries to limit their negative influence. This second step is critical to find balance in your mind and feel happier in yourself, which is what this exercise is all about.

INNER CRITIC EXERCISE:

Think about your inner critic. Give him or her a persona and a name and describe them in detail. What gender are they? What are they wearing? When do they shout and what do they nag you about? Does your inner critic remind you of someone? If so, who?

What is your first memory of your inner critic? When did the voice start showing up? How old were you? What did you experience? How did you feel?

Write down what you would like to say to your inner critic in a few sentences, explaining the impact their negativity has on you. Do not stop until you have exhausted the list of transgressions.

When your inner critic is talking to you, what comes up for you in your body? Do your shoulders tense? Does your heart race? Does your brow furrow? As you notice what your body is feeling, create space to cry—and even yell—out this pain.

This voice has been with you a long time and has an emotional charge, so creating a cathartic moment is important to clearing and reprogramming. Do not proceed until you take this action. Take a deep, cleansing breath, acknowledge your inner critic, and state your boundary.

For example: "Hello, Marie, I see you, and I am going to take care of you today; however, I am going to take care of myself first. I am not afraid of you. Thank you for your ideas but I don't need them now."

My client John had spent decades battling his inner critic. His inner critic voice got louder and louder as he went through medical school, and he was under increased scrutiny and pressure. During the pandemic, John came to me with a severe case of burnout and was constantly second-guessing himself.

During our sessions together, he completed the inner critic exercises, and we discussed the concept of our false versus true selves as well as the importance of taking small steps toward finding his true self. This brought up a lot of anxiety in John for he was so used to doing what was expected of him he struggled with leaning into the idea of trusting himself. By having ongoing sessions that focused on aligning his wants, behavior, and his actions, he was able to shift his lenses to focus on walking in and leading the path to his own story.

By paying attention to the areas in our lives we second-guess and diving deep into the reason behind why we doubt ourselves, we can learn to develop new skills and shift our focus from an outward barometer to reliance on our internal gauges instead. This in turn will help us to trust ourselves—a skill so vital to forming and living our true selves.

But what happens when we continue to let our inner critic roar and get stuck in an endless spiral of second-guessing ourselves while creating an internal unawareness? In the next chapter, we will explore what happens when we choose to live on autopilot and let life just happen to us. We will examine the impact of living unconsciously and the havoc it can wreak on our lives.

CHAPTER 10

UNCONSCIOUS LIFE

"A life lived of choice is a life of conscious action. A life lived of chance is a life of unconscious creation."

—NEALE DONALD WALSCH

Before crashing and burning, I was at my worst. I would do very odd things like forgetting if I had taken my pills in the morning or wondering if I left the dog outside, or I would put refrigerated items in drawers and clean plates in the refrigerator. I would joke with my friends and family and say, "Do I have dementia?"

At one of my lowest points, I was in the room with my husband having a conversation, and when we were done talking, I turned the light off in the room and left him sitting in the dark. "Hey!" he yelled. "Why did you turn out the light on me?" I walked back into the room shocked I had done it because I didn't remember doing it.

I have hundreds and hundreds of examples of being in an unconscious state for over two years. It got progressively worse when the pandemic happened. When I was at my lowest point, the anxiety became so much I contemplated ending it all. After the light incident with my husband, he asked me, "Honey, are you okay? You seem a little scattered." *Ha!* I laughed inside. Being scattered was the least of my problems. I didn't know what I was doing anymore or who was living my life. I didn't know how to stop. I was on autopilot.

I know I am not unique in these examples. Many, if not most, people drift through life without noticing, and without stopping; they make automatic choices versus conscious choices. Not every type or example of disconnection from life is a dark and potentially suicidal moment. Many of the moments are small ones, like forgetting to turn the stove off, not being able to remember where you parked the car, having difficulty finding your phone.

Dr. Mark Williamson, a sociologist, and philosopher surveyed three thousand people, of which 96 percent admitted to living on autopilot (Bloom 2019). Williamson goes on to say many people settle for what happens to them. They call it being "easygoing" rather than choosing to take control of their lives through their conscious thoughts, beliefs, values, and choices. Often people choose to join the gang rather than stand out as it's more difficult to take a different direction and leave or lead the pack.

Do any of these little things sound familiar to you? Have you ever left the stove on, lost your phone, or left the house in a rush, and then you get to the stop sign and you can't remember where you were going or whether or not you forgot to close the garage door?

My colleague Miriam, a physician, described a time during her burnout when her brain fog was so bad, she would walk into her clinic daily and say to God, "Dear God, if you are there, please don't let me make a big mistake with one of my patients." Miriam shared she felt this worry worsened her burnout because she was afraid she was going to make a mistake so large it could cost someone their life.

During my interview with Dr. Jennie Byrne, a brain and behavior expert physician, she explained why this happens in our brains. "Human nervous systems are designed to be coded patterns because they offload the glucose needed to run the body. For example: when you learn how to walk, or you learn how to ride a bike, at first it's really hard. It takes a lot of work. It takes a lot of glucose. It's very effortful, but then it becomes encoded in a pattern in your nervous system. When it is on automatic, you divert your energy stores to other parts of your nervous system. The body is designed to get patterns and then put them on autopilot because it's a way to keep your energy reserved. We tend to do this because it helps us. When it hinders us is when all of your brains are on autopilot."

WHAT IS AN UNCONSCIOUS LIFE VERSUS CONSCIOUS LIFE?

In Tonya's article "How to Live Consciously in an Unconscious World" in *Your Aha! Life*, she states, "To live unconsciously means you are living life without awareness—a lack of awareness of yourself or others. It's to live without knowing who you are, what you want in life, and what matters most to you and to drift along passively in life accepting what comes your way regardless of if it's serving you or others in this world."

If I am being honest, once I identified I suffered from burnout, I struggled with shifting toward living a conscious life. I had been stuck in the "I shoulds" merry-go-round for so long I couldn't get past those old patterns of behavior. I had to deliberately create and build in steps for myself to follow to actively engage my brain, heart, and body at the same time. The steps took time to build and involved a lot of trial and error until I found steps that 1) worked for me and 2) could fit easily into my life without a lot of extra work.

To live consciously means to be awake and alive. "In simple words to live consciously means...that you're creating your life consciously rather than drifting along passively. It means you are aware of your true desires and you're able to direct your energy for the progressive realization of those desires" (Team Soul 2018).

Because I was a driver and overachiever prior, in this new life I was creating, I had to force myself to slow down and rest more. When I noticed I was driving myself too hard or working too much I would stop and reassess what I was experiencing at the moment. If I was tired, I would take a nap. If I was feeling overwhelmed, I would adjust my schedule by eliminating or consolidating meetings or commitments.

SHIFTING FROM UNCONSCIOUS TO CONSCIOUS LIVING

Here are some of the steps I created for myself to help you build some new patterns in your daily life. These are bite-sized, deliberate steps to help you form new habits and routines while providing check-ins so you can easily get back on track if you stumble along the way.

1) BECOME MORE SELF-AWARE

Set aside some time a few times a week for some self-inquiry exercises. Ask yourself what is important to you and what you want. Notice the messages you're telling yourself, note the ones you believe, and notice what gets your attention. You can become more self-aware through journaling, reflecting, and working with a coach or therapist to increase your self-awareness.

2) EXAMINE YOUR TIME AND ENERGY LEVELS

Pick one day a week when you examine your time and energy levels. Ask yourself what routines or habits control your days? Are there things you'd want to change in your routine if they aren't working? Create a daily routine or follow a habit tracker app like *Most Days* on the App store.

3) REFLECT AND ASSESS YOUR IMPACT

Think about how your words, decisions, and actions impact others. Are you aware of the choices and consequences of your actions and behavior? What impact do you make at work, in your community, etc.?

4) FOCUS ON THE NOW

It's impossible to live consciously when you're constantly distracted. Find time to be still and silent and try activities where all three components of your life are engaged at the same time: mind, body, and spirit.

5) OBSERVE THE LITTLE THINGS

For one week write down what you notice when you eat and drink and how what you eat affects your mind and body. Are you aware of the small things and interactions you have with others around you, your kids, your partner, etc.? Notice how you show yourself love—or don't.

As you begin to practice these five steps and incorporate them into your life, you will find your self-awareness will expand, and your consciousness will shift. By shifting from living an unconscious life to a conscious one, you are much closer to reaching an extraordinary life.

In the next chapter, we will explore what you will experience on the other side of living a conscious life and how to communicate with the people in your life you know you can count on and trust. By taking the time to organize your thoughts and words using the prompts above, you can practice having these conversations in a safe space until you become more comfortable sharing with your larger community. In the next chapter, we also explore the importance of building a community of emotional support people to help support you as your journey unfolds.

CHAPTER 11

EMOTIONAL SUPPORT PEOPLE (ESPS)

"Babe, can you just be done? You are so unhappy. It makes me so sad to see you this unhappy. It breaks my heart."

Those words from my husband rocked me to my core. Not only was I breaking my own heart by unconsciously living the life I was existing in—an ordinary life—but I was also hurting someone I loved as well.

I wish I could tell you I walked away from my old life on my own accord, but that's simply not the truth. The truth is my body chose for me. It forced me to change for my health and for those I love and who loved me enough to tell me the truth.

Isn't that what life's all about? Choosing to live a life we love with people we love and those who love us?

Hearing Peter's words and seeing the collateral damage my previous choices were having on him as well as my own body was a hard pill to swallow. Peter and I had been married for fourteen years at this point, and he had seen me crash and burn so many times he lost count. My workaholic nature was something we had joked about on and off for years, and when he observed that my health often rode in the back seat of my life, he would gently mention it to me. I would be defensive, often exploding or yelling, and he would retreat. Through my actions, I reinforced that those gentle nudges weren't welcome. I silenced my body, and I silenced him.

This was the first time in fourteen years I allowed myself to listen and lean into the notion "What if Peter is right? Why can't I just be done?"

Peter loved me enough to break through my bullshit and lay it all out on the line. He was permitting me to not have it all figured out. He was asking me to let go, and I am so glad I did. I am so glad he spoke up, and I am proud of myself that I dared to let go.

As my journey unfolded and as I spoke with many of my clients, so many of them struggled with the details around communicating with partners, family members, and the community about their burnout and the life changes they were going through. The sticking point seemed to always be "Where do I start? What will they say?" We talked about the importance of sharing what you are going through but also the power of timing and listening carefully to what others are saying to you.

WIDENING OUR LENSES

The support systems in our lives often help us with widening our senses and seeing what we don't see. They watch us as we fumble as we head toward our crash and burn moments before we do. They notice our energy levels and our snippy tones. They experience us hurting and acting out our hurt through our actions, and they suffer the consequences. They are along for the ride. They are the passengers in our lives. But there often is a time when they need to step up and become the driver. These are the moments we need to listen.

My colleague Matt shared: "I would come home every night and be so grumpy with my family. My kids would avoid me because the interactions with me became negative." His partner spoke to him one night as they were going to bed and shared with him that the kids kept asking, "Why is Daddy so miserable?" Matt said this was the moment he realized his decision to live in the status quo wasn't working for him anymore. He called a family meeting the next day and they talked through their feelings and their ideas and came up with a plan for Matt to be happy again. They even called it "Daddy's happiness project."

By Matt being open to having the conversation, hearing his family's feedback, and being honest with them about what was happening to him internally, they were able to confront the behavior, acknowledge the hurt and develop a plan they could all contribute to.

These conversations can also spark new insights about how others in our lives are feeling and experiencing the world from their perspectives. Often these conversations can unearth and shed light on the untruths and assumptions we've been telling ourselves for years.

My client Rob is a perfect example of this. Rob had been a doctor for over fifteen years with the same healthcare company. He reached his breaking point during the pandemic. He suffered in silence for a year, not telling anyone how much he hated going to work. He channeled his anger into drinking more in the evening.

During one of our sessions, I encouraged him to journal his feelings and share them with his wife. After completing my suggestion, he texted me and said: "I did it! She listened! She was feeling unhappy too. We agreed I would take some time off and she would go back to work. She has missed working, and I never knew because she never said anything."

So often we think we know what someone we love wants, but if we haven't asked or if they don't tell us differently, we assume. When we do this, we both lose. Rob is now working toward starting a podcast for other healthcare workers. His wife has returned to work and is enjoying her new job as a director of marketing for a start-up.

Asking for help is where so many of us get stuck, and as my burnout recovery journey unfolded, I learned almost daily about the importance of this. Not only did I learn how to ask for help, but I also learned who I could go to for help and when. I called these people my emotional support people. My

ESPs! Honestly, I wouldn't have made it without these people to lean on as going through a transformation can be difficult and lonely at times and you need support from people to help you on your journey.

Rob dared to share his very personal internal dialogue with his wife, allowing the two of them to share their unique vulnerable perspectives and creating a sense of intimacy, a space for them to work together to form a better plan that worked for both of them. Rob allowed himself to be vulnerable, ask for help, and in turn, find his extraordinary. Through his growth, his wife also dared to find hers. Being honest and up-front can reinforce that help is on the way.

When my husband Peter shared his concerns with me, he not only offered me a lifeline but also permitted me to let go. He chose to bet on me, and we leaped together. When I started to return to my old patterns of workaholism or second-guessing myself, he held me accountable and stayed steadfast to his mantra of "I believe in *you*."

When Matt's partner shared with him that their kids noticed he was miserable, he told him the truth. Then they sat together as a family and solved the problem. The truth set them all free, and now the kids have two happy parents, and they have been shown what it looks like to choose joy over sorrow.

Reaching out to your ESPs isn't always about having deep conversations and doing serious personal work. It can also be to celebrate the completion of a goal or be just because. One of my favorite stories came from my client Mark. He had been struggling with feeling unmotivated and unsupported. Together we made a plan for him to build celebration into his life. He needed to include a person who had contributed to him completing his goal. The assignment was life-changing for him. It allowed him to solidify previous relationships and make new friends along the way. It stretched him in ways he never thought possible, and it increased his motivation and support system in his life.

This is an example of how stretching outside of your comfort zone and asking people to come alongside you in your journey makes it so much more enjoyable along the way.

As you read these stories, do any of them resonate with you?

By leaning on others and turning outward enough to trust those supportive people in your life, you give others the chance to be the light for you. Sure, it is scary—if I am honest, it's downright terrifying at times—but every single person I interviewed for *Hello, Head, Meet Heart* agrees that the moment they chose to ask for help and lean on others, it changed their lives.

FINDING YOUR ESPS

As you move along in your journey, one of the most important steps is to create your personal board of directors you can count on to guide you. I have created five questions for you to think through who the best people would be to support you at the right time. Take a moment and jot down your responses.

- Who can I count on to hold me accountable?
- Who can I problem-solve with?
- Who can I celebrate with?
- Who will tell me the truth when I need it?
- Who can I call when I need advice?

These could be different people or the same person/people for each question. For me, I learned early on who was the most helpful for me at which time and in each situation.

Tip: Be sure you choose the people in your life who tell you the truth and who don't tell you solely what you want to hear.

As your journey evolves, you will want to review this list, continue to edit it, and refine it. To get started, you will want to schedule some time with your ESPs, share the goal you chose with each of them, tell them why you chose them and for what category, and most importantly, ask them if they would be willing to help you reach your goal. I give this as homework to many of my clients, and they find their ESPs are excited to hear about how they can help.

Now that we've discussed the importance of asking for help, who to ask for help, and how to ask them, let's examine how we can take the key learnings from the dialogue and feedback we've received from our ESPs and apply those learnings to sharpen our skills and begin to bet on ourselves for the journey to come. We will explore "betting on yourself" in the next chapter.

CHAPTER 12

BETTING ON YOURSELF

"You destroyed a life I was building for someone else so I could finally begin to build a life for me."

—*SIMU LIU*

In 2020 during the pandemic, my colleague Matt had the best financial years he ever had as a business owner, but his personal life was in shambles. For the past two decades, Matt had been killing himself at work in his career in healthcare, but he realized what he'd been doing for the last twenty years was not fulfilling him inside any longer.

He was working ten to twelve-hour days, missing his kids' games and social interactions, and he was missing the intimacy he formerly had with his partner. He was so fed up with his life. He had begun researching and thinking about what he could do to revive the creative portion of his brain. He felt stuck. The biggest barrier to him quitting his lucrative job to do something more fulfilling was keeping the lights on and achieving the monetary incentives he had been achieving in his current role.

Matt didn't know exactly what he wanted. He just knew the life he was living wasn't tenable for him or his relationship any longer. At his darkest moment, he decided to reach out for help and hire a life coach. Together they created a plan for Matt to learn to change his mind-set and reach for his extraordinary. This was the fulfilling life he had dreamed of for so long.

Matt shared with me how his perspective has changed since he hired a life coach. He used to think paying the bills first was most important followed only then by doing what made him happy. Since recovering from burnout and working on changing his mind-set, he has reordered his priorities. He does what makes him happy first and uses money as a tool second. Money is no longer the driver in his life, and now he feels freer. He is currently in the transformation process of leaping from healthcare operations to a more creative retail sales lens by opening three pop-up holiday stores. Matt bet on himself and it's paid off.

Matt's story made me think of my own as we had so many parallels and similarities between our two stories. My betting on myself moment was the moment when I filed the paperwork to start my company SheShatters. Seeing the LLC legal paperwork in black and white was a pivotal step for me to close the door to my past self. I was no longer an employee;

I was an employer. I listened to my heart. I aligned both my head and heart, which gave me the confidence to jump head-first, knowing I was now in charge of my destiny and path.

The jump headfirst was exciting, but it was also scary. Choosing to take the leap of faith to leave an untenable situation is a risky move. It requires you to walk out of one door and enter a new one not knowing what is on the other side. Most often you don't take the leap until the hope for something deeper calls to you louder than it has ever before, and the voice becomes stronger and stronger, pulling you out of the uncomfortable and ordinary life you were living.

My interviews with these gamblers have highlighted that it's quite common for them to have replaced their old-school planning habits instead with faith, and they created their own luck. These gamblers give themselves grace. They shift their internal narratives to focus more on what fulfills them versus what world views would make them successful or deliver what was expected of them.

My colleague Allyson shared that she leaped by betting on herself. "I had to let go. I had to trust in myself, and I have a very strong faith in God. If I stayed in a state of misery, nothing good could come from it. If I make space for the things I say I want, they just start to show up. In my twenties I wasn't prepared to have a big life. I didn't even know what a big life meant.

"For me, it was such a shift of being committed to living a creative life. When I see a creative and fulfilling life, I see one where I'm not only using my gifts in the world but am also still able to balance them with my family and not live in extremes, which was my go-to pattern in the past. I am now committed to living a creatively fulfilling life on my terms, where I can create the dreams I want to happen."

SIZING UP YOUR BET

Betting on yourself requires you to have faith in yourself and hope that your world will be receptive to you leaping into the unknown. It also requires a well-thought-out strategy and a thorough decision-making process.

Matt sized up his bet by meeting with his life coach and husband to talk through how much money he would need to save to take the leap from making a full-time healthcare salary to the risk of earning unsteady income in owning a retail store. He also created a strong business plan, which had a built-in backup plan. My client Allyson's strategy to size up her bet was similar and well-planned-out. She and her husband agreed she would work full-time and start writing her book on the side until she received a steady income stream from her part-time gig.

Before you decide to take your leap, you will want to size up your bet and gather a little more information about whether or not to choose to leap. Here are some questions you will want to explore and answer for yourself:

- If you knew you could not fail, what would you start doing today?
- What qualities do you have that you are confident about?
- What are you good at?

- What can you count on yourself to do?
- What do you need to have financially in place to transition to this new venture part-time or full-time?

Once you explore some of these questions, you may find they are difficult to answer. Please know the questions are designed for you to think through, set aside, and then come back to. You may find you can answer a few of them, but you may need to do some additional research or seek support from a coach, therapist, or trusted resource to ensure you are ready to make the bet and take the leap.

BECOMING THE CEO OF YOUR OWN LIFE

I have wanted to be a CEO since I was seven years old. My best friend Katie and I started our first business when we were in elementary school. We had a garage sale business, and I was in charge of operations and marketing. She was in charge of the money. Fast forward thirty-five years later we are both living the roles we dreamed up for ourselves.

Our journeys were not straight lines to get here. We encountered a lot of trial and error, exploring, pivoting, discovering, and unearthing. What I didn't know then but know now is that there were so many roads I could have taken to becoming a CEO, and the first step was to become the CEO of my own life.

One of the biggest pieces in putting together your life's puzzle is learning how to harness becoming the CEO of your own life. In essence, you begin by starting to discover how you want to live your life. To put these pieces of the puzzle together, you must ask yourself: What do I want to do for a living? What type of work do I want to do? Who do I want to work for? What type of boss do I want or need? Do I want to be my own boss?

As you go through this transition in your life, now is the time to put yourself in the driver's seat. If you feel a sense of resistance to doing this, remember: "If you don't like where you are, change it! You're not a tree." (Rohn 2013).

We all have aspects of our lives we'd like to change. But how many of us do anything about them? Eckhart Tolle eloquently said: "If you cannot make peace with/accept, find enthusiasm for or align with something in your life, it's time to make a change."

I've done my best to do this over the last few years. I've also been brutally honest with myself about what I want and need. Sometimes our current situation doesn't meet our needs, and we want more. But what stops us from making a change? Fear. We ask ourselves: "What if I leave and X happens? I've invested so much time and energy into this. What if I'm insane to want something more?"

The truth is: We outgrow things. We outgrow people and places. What once felt right, might not feel right anymore. It doesn't make us bad, wrong, or weak to realize this. What will weaken us is staying in a situation we can't align with. It's death to the soul. It may be easier to keep going in our routines and stick with what we know, but if we stay, knowing deep down it's not right or even good for us, we exist but aren't fully living.

The way I see it, if you're not happy with something in your life, you have three options:

- stay stuck, resentful, and do nothing
- change your perspective and look for what you can accept, enjoy, and align with in your circumstances
- make a change

A voice in your head might be telling you, *What's the point? There are no better jobs/companies/people out there. Better the devil you know than the devil you don't.*

But the voice is lying to you. Better *does* exist. It *is* out there. But if you don't look for it you will *never* find it.

You might not be able to make the change today or tomorrow. But with a plan, patience, persistence, courage, and time, you can make the changes you need. You may have no idea what the future holds, but know if you don't make a change, nothing will change. Whether you choose to stay stuck or choose to move, both will be uncomfortable. Only with action will you create the change you want and find whatever you seek.

My friend Mary believes becoming the CEO of your own life starts with the simple act of knowing yourself and your values. She believes you need to spend time learning about yourself and exploring areas you are curious about. She says, "I often tell people the dots always connect looking back, never looking forward. You need to follow your interests and follow your passions because that's where creativity comes from. It's how you live your best life."

Talking with Mary made me reflect on my desire as a seven-year-old girl to be a CEO. I had no idea the price I would have to pay to reach such a huge career goal. I was only thinking about how cool it would feel to be in charge of something special as that was how success in life had been defined for me by society.

Since stepping away from my career and choosing to bet on myself, my new definition of a CEO aligns more with Mary's. A true CEO for me now is someone who knows who they are and what they stand for. I have come to learn once you know who you are and what you stand for, the next step is reaching for what you want. The step after is to get it. But how do you get what you want? It all starts with strategizing and creating a plan.

In the next chapter, we will explore what comes next after betting on yourself. We will learn *how* to make a solid plan to keep you focused on your north star as you move along your journey.

CHAPTER 13

MAKING A PLAN

"We must accept the end of something to begin to build something new."

—UNKNOWN

Once I decided to leave my twenty-year career, a huge sense of relief came over me. I simply felt myself unravel from the tight knot I had bound myself in. I felt a sense of peace in knowing I was making the right decision, but I was also scared shitless.

I vacillated between moments of panic and moments of release. My moments of panic came from fear of the unknown and losing the safety and security of a paycheck.

Because I was invested emotionally in the patients, the staff, and the projects I was working on, I gave six weeks' notice. The hardest part was telling my coworkers and the patients I had worked with over the past nine years. I called more than fifty people to share my personal decision to leave. The support I received was astounding. You would have thought I won the lottery. Each person told me they would leave as well if they could. Hearing this was validating yet sad. We were supposed to be the best of the best in the healthcare industry, and we were all just barely surviving. Our sanity was in tatters from the ricochet of COVID.

Leaving one life behind to start anew caused a huge gap in my world. I started to freak out! Because my comfort zone had always been to have a structure in my life, I found it extremely helpful to craft a transition plan for what my new life would look like.

I spent most of my twenties and thirties following a life plan society had crafted for me. I worked my butt off in each company, going back to school to earn my MBA, promotion after promotion, and earning a bigger salary each year. Our society ingrained in me from a young age the principle of money plus status equals happiness. I was following the plan and because I was a good soldier, and I was at the top of my game. I had a nice house, a European brand car, a large bank account balance, the designer doodle dog, and a second vacation home. But…inside I was miserable. I had a yearning inside me for something deeper. My inner voice said to me: *Something bigger is out there for you.*

Creating a plan provided some relief for me to know I was building a new framework for myself, and I had control of it. The life I was building was mine. The life I was living was my choice.

I crafted my plan from the inside out by starting with small steps. Each day I planned to focus on three things: mind, body, and spirit.

To recover and regain my physical health after so many years of self-neglect and per doctors' orders, I needed to ensure I stayed active. I created a fun music playlist and worked out every day. To hold myself accountable for the mind, body, spirit plan, I went to Paper Source (my favorite stationery store) and bought myself a beautiful gold embellished notebook. The notebook had a tiny bumblebee on the front with the message below: "Do something creative every day." This quote resonated with me, so I made a list of active, creative things I liked to do and wanted to explore.

To focus my mind and continue my growth, I read one book a week and listened to one new podcast a week. To complete this goal, I decided to tactically pose the question to my Facebook and LinkedIn community: "What is one book or podcast you would recommend?"

I also researched start-ups, female founders, and organizations I admired, and I asked them to have virtual coffee with me to learn more about them and their stories. I studied these entrepreneurs and learned more about them as founders and the communities they served.

To keep my spirit engaged and to keep me energized, I started writing again along with drawing and coloring. I started designing and creating my new logo, website, and brand. I signed up for Pinterest and made mood boards. I bought myself a small bouquet and arranged them to add some color and joy to my life.

These small steps kept me moving forward toward the creation of my new life. I was no longer running away from something; I was forging ahead toward the yearning for something I could not yet fully see.

As I began to talk with other people in my community, I realized the importance of having and making a plan.

My colleague Allyson shared that during her life transition, making a plan to build the foundation for her new life was a crucial step for her to engage in and trust the new life she wanted for herself was possible—not just a dream.

During COVID Allyson was working in HR and coaching but she had wanted to be a Broadway actress for over two decades. Years before she had received some painful but direct feedback that the timing just wasn't right for her. During COVID she had a creative crisis brought on by her grandmother's passing. Inspired and on the side, Allyson started writing a musical about her grandmother's life. Allyson decided to block out times in her week to start writing and explore this new path. As she shared her writing with her family and community, the feedback she received was incredible. Allyson found she loved the creative process of writing and composing her music. Allyson was an artist, and she was now living out her dream. It worked out better than she could have ever imagined.

Once Allyson could see this new dream was possible, she reached out to her then-life coach, who helped her make a plan to leave HR and ramp up her coaching business. She estimated how much money she would need to save to quit her HR job and make the leap toward living her full-time dream. "I created a plan to work through my fear and determined what my exit plan would be…it wasn't like I just jumped. It was very methodical."

Having a tangible and methodical plan to step into a new transition is key to moving forward, but it is also helpful in preventing you from moving backward.

One of my biggest fears in walking away from my old life was recreating those negative patterns in my new one. To avoid this as much as possible, I crafted a Burn Bright Action Plan. This plan consisted of me setting a larger goal and then key tactics to complete my goal. I made a list of questions for myself. What did I need to start doing to achieve my goal? What did I need to stop doing? I examined what was working for me so far to reach each set goal and then I made a list of what people I needed to ask for support from to help me meet each goal.

When I came up with the idea for a company (SheShatters) devoted to helping professionals heal from burnout and build meaningful, extraordinary lives, I knew I couldn't do this alone. I needed help designing this, so I reached out to my community of friends, family members, and previous colleagues to interview them about how the last couple of years had been for them. I asked for them to share their stories of burnout, specifically what they needed help with. The long list of items unfolded. It was overwhelming.

Knowing I had a big task ahead of me, I reached out for support from people I'd worked with in the past. I reached out to Paty, a former intern, and asked if she would be willing to help me on the side. I also reached out to my niece Rachel, a dynamo in sales and marketing. I thought she would be extremely helpful with the website marketing side of things. Together the three of us assembled a small team, and I began to research branding agencies who would be a good fit for my mission and vision moving forward. I knew how important branding and marketing would be to the core of my business. I started to put my MBA to work and leaned on the business plans, the strengths and weakness analysis formula, and all of the tools I had learned in the twenty-six months of my MBA program.

Finally, the pieces were coming together. My MBA wasn't just a three-letter accessory anymore. It was much more. I felt like all the pieces were coming together. All my coaching, consulting, marketing, personal relations, and experience of the last twenty years were aligned. This was my moment to prove to myself I could bet on myself, and I was worth betting on. To solidify this idea, the last puzzle piece I needed to put in place was to choose a company name. After talking with my supportive network of past colleagues, loved ones, and friends, we decided on the name—SheShatters.

As the company started to form, I quickly realized designing tools and resources for burned-out professionals wasn't going to be enough. Yes, we needed help to heal from burnout but then what? What did life look like after burnout? We needed an avenue for our community to learn new ways of being and how to step into a new life post-burnout. My solution: to create a podcast focusing on conversations with real women and men on how to keep their flames alive—in essence, how to keep professionals motivated to change their habits, not fall into their old patterns, and instead learn *how* to burn bright.

BURNOUT PREVENTION PLAN

For many of us who have experienced burnout, it isn't a one-time occurrence. Often people who experience burnout will burn out again if they do not determine the root cause of their burnout and how to prevent it. Creating a burnout prevention plan helps us identify our goals, our triggers, and what type of support we need in our lives to avoid those burnout patterns in our lives.

Below is the burnout prevention plan I created to help you along your journey:

1) Pick one goal you want to work on that will provide you with some relief today in your life. This can be work-related, a personal goal such as living more fully in your joy, creating more art, or taking a class. It can also be a physical goal—eat lunch, take a break, and sleep X hours a night. Or it can be a relationship goal—connect more with myself or my partner, walk in nature, repair a damaged relationship, set clearer boundaries, or ask for what I want. It can be whatever you want it to be. This is for you.

To complete your plan, you'll write your one goal at the top and answer the following questions:

- What do you want to *stop* doing to achieve your goal?
- What do you want to *keep* doing that's working for you?
- What do you want to *start* doing?
- When are you going to *ask* for help when you get off track with your goal?
- What are the signs you're meeting this goal?
- How are you going to *celebrate* when you've accomplished this goal?

After you complete your plan, here are some reflective questions to ask yourself:

- Did you have challenges with picking a goal or narrowing it down to one?
- What did you find was the most challenging category? The stop, keep, or start?

As you ponder the answers to these deep questions, it is normal if worry or fear starts to creep in for you. If you look at your answers, you might even start feeling scared and overwhelmed. It is important to pause and acknowledge ending an old chapter in your life is painful and scary, even if it feels like the right thing to do. Making a solid plan will keep you focused and accountable to create a sense of safety and comfort for you as you walk toward your new life.

In the next chapter, we will show you *how* to hard-wire some new habits by unlocking creativity and play in your life.

CHAPTER 14

CREATIVITY AND PLAY

"The creation of something new is not accomplished by the intellect but by the play instinct acting from inner necessity. The creative mind plays with the objects it loves."

—CARL JUNG

About a year before COVID hit, I felt a restlessness I had never felt before. Often at work, I would be sitting at my desk with two phones—one in each ear. I'd listen to two different meetings as I was often double booked during my day at work. Many days I would tune these conversations out, and my mind would wander to dreaming of those moments in my life when I attempted to fill my cup and tap into my aliveness again.

During a particularly hectic week at work, I canceled a few of my meetings one afternoon and took a drive down to my local grocery store, New Seasons. It was a beautiful sunny day, and as I walked into the store, I stopped outside by the floral area. I found myself surrounded by beautiful flowers: dahlias, freesias, gerbera daisies, and tulips. The sweet smell of their aromas enveloped me.

Surprising myself, I started grabbing different stems and different colors. Bunching them together in my hand, I began making a bouquet of tiny, beautiful, colorful things, and my heart immediately felt lighter and fuller. I could feel the anxiety loosen in my shoulders and chest.

I spent a few minutes in this colorful, sensory space, and when I was satisfied with my arrangement, I walked over to the outside checkout stand, and no one was over there. I stood there for a while, and then a woman came up to me and said, "Do you work here? I need help picking out some flowers."

I started to say no, but she looked like she needed help. And I loved arranging flowers, and no one was there. So, I said, "Sure I would be happy to help you arrange a bouquet." So, for the next twenty minutes, this stranger and I worked together to create a lovely bouquet for her mother-in-law's birthday.

As the woman and I talked more, I fessed up and told her I didn't work there. She laughed and she asked me, "So if you don't work here, what do you do for a living?"

I told her I worked in healthcare and had for twenty years, and she said, "So then are you off today?"

And I said: "No, I just couldn't stand my day anymore, so I canceled my afternoon meetings and came here. And then I got stuck in the flower area. And I was enamored with all the colors. And I felt myself come alive."

She chuckled and laughed. "Well, you're certainly good at it. You could do this for a living. You made something really beautiful."

I felt a warmness flow through my body at the compliment she gave me. A yearning tugged at my heart as I missed tapping into the creativity and playful side of myself. My job had beaten the joy out of me. I missed surrounding myself with tiny, beautiful things I loved.

When I got home that night, I told my husband and a few close friends about my "New Seasons experience." They laughed and thought it was funny, but later I couldn't stop thinking about the seed planted in me by one simple stranger's compliment: *You made something really beautiful.*

SPARKING CREATIVITY

After I decided to leave my job, I had so much inner work I needed to do and old patterns I needed to unravel. The inner work was arduous and at times I needed a break to create space to spark creativity and incorporate play back into my life.

I decided to institute a new routine and treat myself to a tiny, beautiful gift or experience once a week. This usually consisted of me going to Target, the local Goodwill, or a local stationery store and purchasing a beautiful writing journal, quote cards, coloring book, or colored pencils. Once a month I would go to New Seasons and design a floral arrangement for myself. Whatever the gift for the week, my goal was to activate the right side of my brain—the creative side. I found that accessing this new part of myself helped me to widen my lenses and realize I was, in fact, a creative and innovative person who hadn't lost the spark in me.

Seeing this potential in myself also made me curious to understand more about the notion of playing versus producing. After spending twenty years in healthcare, such a regulated industry, I had felt the pressure to attach all of my activities to some type of outcome. The thought of even embarking on an activity just for fun or pure enjoyment felt lazy to me. Little did I know when I began to focus on just enjoying and being, that's when my most fantastical ideas flooded in.

I became curious to know why this happens. According to scientific research, the right side of the brain is proven to be the creative side of the brain. This side also controls things like daydreaming, intuition, art, rhythm, and imagination (Allen 2022).

This research made sense to me, and as I started to incorporate new routines into my daily life, I found my thoughts were beginning to shift a little more as well. I was perceiving my current situation differently than I was before, and I was more open to the possibilities of what may lie ahead for me in the future. I was leaning into my creative side and enjoying seeing what I could make by living in the process instead of the outcome.

According to Miriam Reyes in her article "The Right Side of the Brain," the right side of the brain is considered to be the receptor and identifier of spatial orientation and is responsible for the way we perceive the world regarding color, shape, and place. We know we are using the right brain faculties when:

- We feel, perceive, smell, or touch.
- When we imagine.
- When we fantasize.
- When we visualize.
- When we take risks.

People living primarily on the left side of the brain tend to be more quantitative and analytical. They only see parts of the whole picture as they may get lost in the details and are ruled by logic. It is important to spend time accessing and using the right side of the brain as well because the right side of the brain sees and experiences the unity of everything around you, which affects our overall well-being (Wong 2020).

PLAYTIME

As I continued to build creativity into my life, I found my mood was lighter, and I became more playful with my family and friends. It was more fun! I was Hannah again, and the spark inside me was getting stronger.

In the past I had always viewed play as something I didn't have time for—nor did I make room for it because I couldn't rationalize spending the time on something with little to no outcome. The reality was I was only seeing a part of the whole picture.

A *New York Times* reporter, Kristin Wong, described this dilemma well: "One way to think about play is it's an action you do that brings you a significant amount of joy without offering a specific result. This means taking a bike ride because it's fun, not because you're trying to lose five pounds. A lot of us do everything hoping for a result. It's always, 'What am I getting out of this?' The play has no result."

Once I understood the purpose of the play was for me to *feel* something instead of *do* something, that permitted me to explore what real play was for me.

If you're wondering how to access your right brain and lean into those carefree days you had as a child, here's an exercise that helped me narrow down what *play* was for me:

- Think about what you liked to do when you were seven years old.
- What were your favorite ways to play?
- List a few of the activities.
- If you liked to play tether ball, maybe sign up for a tennis lesson.
- If you like gymnastics or dancing, sign up for a dance class or put on music and dance.
- If you loved playing with your model kitchen and making up recipes, take a cooking class.

My client Abby found this exercise helpful for her and her husband. They had been struggling for a while with feeling stuck in their day-to-day monotonous marriage. After doing the play exercise, Abby realized she missed dancing as she had been in gymnastics and dance when she was younger. She signed her and her husband up for ballroom and salsa dancing lessons and they loved it.

Abby got to dance again, and Jim, her husband, learned to both lead and follow the dancing step techniques. This created intimacy and emotional connectedness between the two of them they hadn't ever experienced before.

Abby and her husband were a great example of what can happen when you are feeling lost in your life, marriage, etc. and you lean into each other to share your creative and playful sides and create a more colorful life that you love. In the next chapter, we will explore combining your inner and external worlds to design and create a living, breathing, lasting legacy.

CHAPTER 15

LEARNINGS TO LEGACY

"When you do what is expected of you-you can lose yourself."
—SHARON ATHAS-COTE (MENTOR)

A few months before I decided to quit my job, in a dire moment, I picked up the phone and called one of my mentors—Sharon Athas-Cote. Sharon is a former boss of mine when I worked at the *Alaska Magazine/Milepost Advertising* agency in high school, and I have known her for thirty years. She is a dynamo, owning her own construction company, which primarily deals with governmental contracts. Sharon is a bulldog and takes no shit from anyone, but she has the kindest heart of anyone I know. Every year she sends me a note on Valentine's Day in the mail that simply says: "I love you."

If I want the real hard truth, I call Sharon. When Sharon answered, I filled her in on my mini midlife crisis. I went on and on, and afterward, I asked her what I should do. She got quiet, which is never a good thing, and I knew she was going to unleash the truth. "Hannah, you've been wanting to quit since last year and the year before. Shit or get off the pot. Just freaking *do it!*"

I immediately threw out a bunch of excuses. I could not just quit without another job to go to. What would I do? How would I make money? Was I crazy to leave a twenty-year career I had worked so hard for?

Sharon got quiet again. *Ugh, the double whammy was coming. I could feel it.*

"Hannah, I don't know how to say this, but when you first went into healthcare and chose the leadership and management track, I was shocked. I thought you would do something bigger, more in line with your spirit. I'm not saying I'm disappointed in you because you have been successful, but I always thought you were destined for more."

Her words penetrated my soul. I felt them internalized in my bones, my skin. They were the words I'd been telling myself quietly for years. *I am wasting my life. More is out there for me.* She was quiet, letting the words steep between us. I was rocked. She had spoken the words out loud I never allowed myself to utter. Wow. Sharon truly *saw* me, and she loved me enough to speak the words out loud, for the cost of not doing so would have been reckless for both of us.

As I think of that memory, I can now see throughout my career I have been blessed to have several mentors in my life. These mentors are from all different walks of life and are of different genders, and races and the one thing they all have in common is they want me to be the best version of myself and to find true joy. They are also brutally honest with me.

We find mentors in all aspects of our lives—in our work, our community, and often in our families. Mentors impact our lives in many ways.

They can:

- *help us relate to ourselves with mindfulness and compassion as people on a journey in progress*
- *inspire us with examples of how/where we would like to evolve, personally and professionally*
- *give us the straight truth about what's holding us back and how we can course-correct along the way*
- *give us both global lessons and sometimes specific tools for moving forward*
- *help us let go of excuses or self-limiting beliefs and find our creativity and boldness*

That day Sharon gave me the straight truth about what and who was holding me back. She gave me the support and confidence to course-correct at that pivotal moment in my life.

Our family members can often be impactful mentors for us. My colleague Danielle credits her mom as a huge mentor in her life. She describes her mom as unbelievably brilliant, entrepreneurial, and a very generous but take-charge woman.

Seeing her mother exhibit these qualities inspired Danielle to emulate them. Danielle grew up surrounded by generosity, the idea that business is personal, who you are and what actions you take influences others, and you can do what you love. Danielle's mom inspired her to adopt an entrepreneurial spirit and the courage to evolve both professionally and personally.

Our mentors can often be our peers. My client Emily says her mentors are commonly other entrepreneurial founders of start-ups. By being in the company of these incredible founders, she learned the importance of being curious and exploring those things in life that interest her.

"Whenever I ask one of my mentors why they started their company, they always say, 'I was interested in exploring more about...'" By surrounding herself with mentors who emphasize and promote growth and curiosity, Emily is constantly learning and experiencing new things that challenge her self-limiting beliefs. This group of people encourages her to step into her power and boldness.

WHEN MENTORS AREN'T PEOPLE: THE "SHOULD HAVES"

Our mentors aren't always people. They can be the things we're most regretful about, and often they can be the best teachers. When I started to forge the path toward my new life, I made a list of things I should have done differently. The purpose of this exercise for me was to reflect on what I learned from the last twenty years in my career and avoid making the same mistakes again.

Initially, I did the exercise just for me, but as I built my company and started speaking to companies about burnout prevention and sharing my experiences with others, I found I could use those things I regretted doing or not doing as teaching lessons. To do this, I had to turn toward myself and examine what responsibility I owned in each situation. Looking at my actions through a new lens, I identified where I needed to accept responsibility for my part in the situation and where I chose to shift the blame to avoid feeling the shame and regret of my actions.

A surprising outcome of this exercise was the opportunity for me to turn the "should haves" into "will dos" going forward. Then I turned the "will dos" into gifts for others—tiny gifts of knowledge and advice to share with someone in my life that they could use to build their legacy.

TURNING LEARNING INTO LEGACY

"What brings you joy?" My spiritual guru asked me this question during my time at the retreat center and in many ways, the answer has led me to where I am now. When I knew I was done with my previous work life, but I couldn't trust myself to stop working for fear of the unknown path ahead, the excavation of all my old patterns helped me rediscover myself. In essence, I was learning to choose joy over fear.

Throughout my life, I hadn't thought about what the definition of joy was to me. I had mostly strived for success that was more outcome-based and had a tangible outcome to me versus a feelings-based concept. As I thought about the concept of joy, I realized I was so used to being busy and getting swept up in the frenetic energy of life, I had never fully paid attention to my moments of joy as I was always living in the future instead of the present.

After going through the incredible journey of breaking, healing, and then bouncing back, I realized my definition of joy was what I was living now—a feeling of contentment and delight. I was lit up from the inside out. I was relying on my internal world instead of relying on the external world to create the feeling of joy.

For all the barriers to joy and happiness—fear, the inner critic, layers of *"shoulds,"* the relentless need to be busy and productive—we have many more reasons to pursue joy and ultimately create our own story and lasting legacy.

My friend Lisa is an example of this. Lisa worked in the corporate world for several decades, thinking she was searching for true happiness by looking for it in the external facets of life—money, status, and material belongings. When COVID hit, she described herself as having a mini midlife crisis moment.

During lockdown, Lisa realized what she had been searching for externally had been locked inside her all along. It just needed to get out. A few months later, she decided to walk away from her corporate career and pivot toward a career in the art world, something that had brightened her joy in her early thirties.

"When you follow joy, and you believe in yourself enough to walk away from something that other people have created for you, those societal expectations, you can achieve anything you want. The ultimate sacrifice you make is by looking after yourself first then you can look after others."

Lisa and I weren't the only examples of women choosing to step into joy, share our learnings and create a lasting legacy for ourselves and others.

My colleague Allyson is a high-level HR executive at one of the biggest firms in New York. In her twenties, her dream was to be an actress and to make it on Broadway. While she was working in HR she was auditioning for shows and cabarets, but she wasn't getting cast in any roles.

She received some tough feedback from her agent and the acting community that this just wasn't the right time for her to pursue her dream and follow her joy. Based on this feedback, Allyson chose to place her dream on hold, have kids, and attempt to find joy in her HR job. Unfortunately, she found complacency instead of joy.

Fast forward fifteen years. During COVID, Allyson realized she missed being in a creative space, so she began writing a musical in her spare time, which she later turned into a novel. Ultimately, she became a published author. Although she found her joy fifteen years later, Allyson's story about choosing joy over complacency sooner rather than later is trickling down to the next generation—her kids. Allyson is now making choices to live in joy and leave a lasting legacy for her kids and the next generation.

DESIGNING YOUR LEGACY

If you're not sure where to start to begin designing your legacy, here are a few questions to get you started:

- Imagine your life has come to an end, and you're assessing it from the outside.
- Summarize in two or three sentences how you want to be known and remembered.
- Does your legacy align with your values?
- What roles or responsibilities do you have currently that directly feed into your vision of a legacy?

Based on the answers to the questions above, begin to write or draw what you would like your legacy to be and list a few ideas you have and steps you need to take to get there. For example: If you want to be a mentor or create a scholarship fund for an organization, you will want to brainstorm ways to raise or save money for the scholarship and outline how much you would need and by when. If you want to mentor others, you will want to start researching organizations to mentor at or identify the specific population you would like to be a mentor for.

Asking yourself these specific questions will help you narrow down and identify clear next steps to turn your ideas into action.

AN UNINTENTIONAL LEGACY

It is important to acknowledge that sometimes we don't get to choose the legacy we leave. It doesn't always come from us making the conscious choice to alter our path. Often lessons come from those unchosen moments when life simply happens.

My client Nicole, a director of people operations at a large healthcare company, is a perfect example of this. In 2016 she was diagnosed with a rare form of cancer with a 2 percent survival rate. After several rounds of stem cell transplant therapy, she found she wanted to share her story with other future cancer survivors.

Determined to fulfill her dream of writing a book and making a difference in others' lives, she started a six-month "launch your dream" book course and took on the challenge. As the book unfolded, she wanted to share learnings with her daughter about the importance of leaning into joy and creating a life you love.

"When I am no longer here, and cancer finally takes me down, the gift I want to give my daughter is the openness to understanding that it's okay for her to take care of herself in a way that works for her. I want her to know I am letting go of my preconceptions about what it means to be doing well or to be successful and say to her instead: 'I'm really glad you are so self-aware that you know what you need to do right now to take care of yourself.' If I share no other message with my kids or leave no other legacy to them, I want them to know they were never alone. I was always there with them."

Nicole, choosing to turn one of the darkest and most unexpected moments in her life into a lesson for future cancer survivors and her kids, is a true example of giving others the tools to move forward even after life ends.

My client Iselyn knows firsthand about the power of sharing one's legacy. Iselyn always wanted to be a children's book author, but she was always afraid to do it. When COVID happened, she realized, *You can't keep waiting for the perfect time. There is no perfect time.*

Her best friend Kelly became ill and died from breast cancer during COVID, and the last thing Kelly said to her was, "You need to do anything and everything you thought you wanted to do because I thought I had time, and I ran out of it. Write the book for me."

The lesson her best friend taught her (that Iselyn is now sharing with her grandkids) is leaning into joy and allowing yourself to go through experiences that satisfy your soul is living a fulfilling life. Don't wait until it's too late.

By Kelly sharing her wish for Iselyn on her deathbed, she created a catalyst within Iselyn and paved the way for her to keep moving forward and reach for joy every day. In return, Iselyn's living legacy to Kelly is this: "If I know I'm getting up every day and I'm moving, whatever the movement is—whether a little step or a big step—I feel fulfilled knowing I'm heading in a direction I've set out to go. I know Kelly is smiling down on me saying, 'You've got this.'"

These powerful stories of mentorship, learning, and legacy made me reflect on what I wanted my legacy to be post-burnout. My previous definition of joy was muddled and unclear, but now, after I had done the difficult inner work to heal myself, it became clearer. It was my turn to mentor, inspire, and teach others how to thrive in their inner lives post-pandemic. Now was the time to be vulnerable and share my life lessons with the world, teaching others how to turn their own life experience into a legacy.

I will show you how to unleash your legacy by stepping into your extraordinary in the next chapter.

CHAPTER 16

STEPPING INTO THE EXTRAORDINARY

"Fear will try to pull you back, but focus on the growth. It will urge you on."

—*HANNAH AUSTIN*

One of the biggest mistakes I made was thinking jumping from my old life (the ordinary) to the extraordinary (my new life) was going to be easy and I could make it happen overnight. I found out very quickly it takes time to unravel old patterns and step out of your old self and your previous life. I realized that before you get to a "destination extraordinary," you have to get to a livable, sustainable, enjoyable, *good* life first.

Getting to a livable life is often where people get stuck and give up. It's even harder work to build an extraordinary life. An extraordinary life costs a "normal" life. You can't have both. This is the defining moment where you will have to sacrifice something you value less than whatever you ultimately want.

Jim Collins, in his book *Good to Great,* said it best: "Good is the enemy of great. That's one of the key reasons why we have so little that becomes great. Few people attain great lives, in large part because it is just so easy to settle for a good life."

It is so true. Many people don't want to give up the comfort of good because it's easy to settle for good. Although it's painful to reach for great, it's worth it in the end, but it's quite a journey to get there.

We have all heard the saying "The journey is everything," which could never be truer than when you are attempting to make a big shift in your life. The tricky thing is you have to begin to build your bridge as you are crossing it. What I mean by that is as you are working toward your new life, you still have to live in the present and now more than ever. You have to pay attention. This is the time for you to explore and experiment with what you like and don't like, what you want to keep doing and stop doing. For many of you, this may mean journaling, making notes, writing down what you are discovering about yourself, and building new habits. For others, it may mean working through your feelings and observations out loud with a trusted person in your life, coach, or therapist.

For my client Jamie, the artist, this meant creating an avatar of herself visually and drawing out how she saw herself surrounded by colors as well as magnetic and artistic people while living near the water instead of the city. By drawing out these images, she was able to see and feel what stepping into a new life for herself could look like.

From there she started mapping out each step per month she would need to take to get to her new self. "I was struggling with figuring out how to get from A to Z, my endpoint. I talked with my art teacher, and she suggested I draw it out. Suddenly the steps became clearer, and as I started mapping out the steps and then taking them on one by one, suddenly it wasn't so overwhelming anymore. My new life was unfolding right before my eyes. I had begun living it."

My client Mandy struggled with being patient and kind to herself during this process. "I knew it was going to take work to shift my patterns of old behavior, but as I started to work through some of those negative patterns, so much family drama and dynamics bubbled up. So I needed to pause and dig deep into the issues I was facing with my mom's alcoholism as well as how it affected me and my entire family. I realized I had so many codependency issues that were holding me back from living the life I wanted to live. I kept trying to force the healing and, in the end, it forced me backward."

Many of us try to force our growth, often limiting us to trust the process and let go. It is important during this time to recognize the signs your body, gut, and heart are showing you. If the voice inside you is telling you to pace yourself and stop pushing, you need to listen. By taking a moment to pause, check in with yourself, and work through things at your own pace, you will find you can heal more fully and live more authentically. There is no rush. The goal is just continued growth.

FEAR

After working with my clients, the concept of fear is one of the biggest hurdles for them to overcome. Fear can distract us. It can lead to excuses and prevent us from moving forward. Often, we get stuck in excuses. They can become our narratives and our truths. However, when we start to believe and live these untruths, we deviate from our extraordinary path and stay stuck on the ordinary one.

My client Angela described the moment when fear overcame her after a conversation with one of her family members. "My mom thought I was crazy for wanting more than a nine-to-five job. When I told them I was going to move to Spain and live my passion to start my writing career, they told me it was unsafe to move during the pandemic, and I wouldn't be able to pay my bills. They were telling me everything that was going to go wrong, and it scared me. I began to second-guess myself. What if they were right?"

Angela's story is a great example of how one conversation can cause our fears and insecurities to resurface. Our loved ones may think they're helping by warning us about what could happen. They might think warning us will keep us safe, but ultimately it can obstruct our intuition. By leaning into the fear and working through it, our gut instinct and intuition can guide us instead.

To examine our fears more closely, in our sessions together, I ask my clients to create a chart of the fear, risk, and rewards in their life. This is similar to a pro and con list. I find putting it down on paper helps us see the situation for what it truly is.

Sometimes it allows us to see that the risks we are considering may not be as risky as we thought after all. Risks don't have to be negative. They are just things that might happen, but they might actually turn out to be positive experiences.

This was true for me. As I stumbled and fell along my path to get to a livable, enjoyable, and sustainable life, I began to discover new things about myself. I learned I enjoyed eating intuitively instead of eating my feelings. I found I preferred moving my body through kayaking, dance, and yoga instead of just hitting the bike or the treadmill.

I discovered many of the people I surround myself with saw me as competition instead of someone to collaborate with. I found the walls I had been putting up around my heart were preventing me from letting true love in. I found I had built a life for someone else through someone else's lens.

Through processing the likes and dislikes, the feelings of anger, sadness, and loneliness, I began to find my livable and enjoyable life. Then and only then could I start to reach for the extraordinary.

SHIFTING FROM LIVABLE TO THE EXTRAORDINARY
It's one thing to know the life you are living isn't working for you any longer and know you want something more.

However, defining your extraordinary is personal, and only you can define it.

As I interviewed people for this book, I asked them, "What does living an extraordinary life mean to you?" I received a myriad of responses, some of which I had never even considered.

- Living an extraordinary life means confronting and resolving all the shit that has happened to me.
- Living an extraordinary life means you are choosing joy over the status quo.
- Living an extraordinary life means that my mind and my heart are open.

Their answers revealed one common theme—the notion that to reach extraordinary, *you* must do the work. *You* must choose to confront that which no longer works and pay attention to the life you currently live. What stands between living an ordinary life versus an extraordinary one? The answer is *you*.

WHAT IS YOUR EXTRAORDINARY?

As you read the responses above, do any of them ring true for you? If not, how would you choose to define an extraordinary life? Do you think it's possible to attain? Do you think you are deserving of one? What would it take for you to reach for your extraordinary?

As you start to think through these questions, you may surmise a good life is good enough for you. If that's the case, that's okay, but if you are still feeling something in your life is missing, let me help you discover what the missing piece is.

HOW TO GET OUT OF YOUR OWN WAY

Many of my SheShatters clients tell me they want a change in their life, but they keep getting in their own way. In essence, they are the roadblocks.

A recent *Forbes* article, "Forty-Eight Ways to Get Out of Your Own Way and Start Making Real, Lasting Change in Your Life," highlighted the sentiment that our greatest obstacle in life is ourselves. "It's not that we can't force ourselves to grit our teeth and push through. It's not that we don't *know* what we should be doing, or how we could better apply ourselves. Self-sabotage happens in small, almost undetectable moments. Our minds breed resistance through repetition."

If this is the case for you, here are some ideas for you to practice removing yourself as the roadblock:

1. Start dreaming in strategy, not theory. Think about *how* you could create or accomplish something, not *if* you could.
2. Research one new thing a week. Read a book or article or listen to a podcast. One impactful sentence you read or hear could help you shift your perspective on what's possible and show you what steps to take to move forward.
3. Start spending as much time as you can with people who already have the life you want.
4. Channel your dissatisfaction into fuel. Let it dare you to create the life you want to be living.

Once you begin to practice these suggested ideas, you will begin to feel more comfortable with leaning into your growth and feel more confident to step into your extraordinary. I know it's terrifying, exciting, and exhilarating all at the same time. Just know I have been there, and I am cheering you on along the way.

CHAPTER 17

THE GODDESS OF NEVER BROKEN

"Until you are broken, you don't know what you're made of."
—*ZIAD K. ABDELNOUR*

As I was writing *Hello, Head, Meet Heart*, I came across an article that rocked me to my core and changed my whole perspective on my seeing myself as broken. The article was titled "Why Lying Broken in a Pile on Your Bedroom Floor Is a Good Idea" (Peters 2021). It resonated with me, and I thought, "*Thank God I'm not the only one who has had a floor moment!*"

I immediately felt a sense of connection and curiosity to keep on reading.

The article began: "You know that feeling when you have just gone through a breakup or lost your job, and everything is terrible and terrifying and you don't know what to do, and you find yourself crying in a pile on your bedroom floor? There is a goddess from Hindu mythology that teaches us that, at this moment, in this pile on the floor, you are more powerful than you've ever been" (Peters 2021).

The last statement hit me hard in my gut. Something cracked open in me, and relief flooded in.

I read on. The article shared the goddess's name—Akhilandeshvari. The origin of her name in Sanskrit means "goddess" or "female power," and the "Akhilanda" means essentially "never not broken."

Hearing the description of her name brought me back to the moment when I was lying on the bathroom floor contemplating ending it all. At that moment I viewed myself as "weak." But now through the lens of this article, I could see it wasn't a moment of failure for me. It was simply a moment of changing course.

Lying in a pile on the floor was an acknowledgment that things were so dark I just couldn't go on the way I had before. This new realization allowed me to let go of the "failure narrative" that I had been labeling myself with for so long. A new thought bubbled up. I wasn't broken. I was simply turning toward a wound in me that would later let the light in.

By surrendering to the moment on the floor, I was acknowledging the life I was living wasn't working for me. That was the time to sift through the reality of my current life, sort through the components to see which were worthy of keeping and discard the rubble that no longer fit.

With the new realization I wasn't broken, a new visual formed in my mind. What if I was already whole, but my wholeness was a jumbled puzzle, and the secret to locking my pieces together was to let go, explore, and find new pieces that fit.

Turning back to the article I read on. "Now is the time, this time of confusion and brokenness and fear and sadness, to get up on the fear, ride it down to the river, dip into the waves, and let yourself break. Become a prism. All the places where you've shattered can now reflect light and color where there was none. Now is the time to become something new, to choose a new whole" (Peters 2021).

The concept of harnessing and choosing to ride my fear was a new mind-set for me. My entire life I was told and shown that fear was something I should stay away from. "Don't touch the stove. It will burn you." "Don't talk with her. She cannot be trusted." "Stay away from that project. It's a losing battle." I know the people in my life had good intentions when they were saying these things. They thought they were helping and keeping me safe. However, the opposite was true because the false sense of "safety" was holding me back. I became stuck, stunted, and cycling in old patterns. I wasn't growing, expanding, or learning.

As I reflected more on this concept, I realized I had let fear control my life. I wasn't rejecting it or using it to propel me. I wasn't harnessing its power. I didn't even recognize it had so much power over me. In this new life I was building for myself, I now had the choice to jump into the fear head-on and explore the space inside it—its crevasses. I could choose to let go, ride the waves of fear, and allow myself to explore my wholeness like the goddess.

As I read the final excerpt of the article, it had one final lesson for me:

"Even in that new whole, that new, colorful, amazing groove that we create is an illusion. It means nothing unless we can keep on breaking apart and putting ourselves together again as many times as we need to. In our brokenness, we are unlimited." (Peters 2021).

This statement brought it full circle for me. For most of my life, I had been focused on fixing things that weren't working and were deemed "broken," including myself. The notion that, even after I worked so hard to start a new life for myself and did the work to become "whole" again, the real beauty and lesson in all of it was that wholeness was never the destination I was reaching for. It was an illusion.

The real beauty was that I learned how to harness the power— the goddess inside me all along.

HARNESSING YOUR INNER GODDESS

As you read my story and reflections, what thoughts and feelings start to bubble up in you? Have you struggled with letting fear control your life? Do you call yourself broken?

The stories we tell ourselves about who we are and what we've been through can be hurtful and damaging to our growth. Those beliefs limit us from reaching our true potential.

As you read this chapter, I want you to start to think about how you can reframe the things you say to yourself in private. I want to challenge you to see yourself the way others and I see you. As you begin to reframe how you see yourself, I want you to visualize yourself on top of a mountain looking back at how far you've come to get right where you are today.

What are those traits, skills, and superpowers only you have? The ones that got you *here*. Look back at those difficult moments you've overcome. Did those experiences teach you something? Are you stronger now than you were before? The answer is *yes*. If you are reading this, you've already done the hard work. You've always known how to harness your inner Goddess. She has always been there. Now is the time to find and harness her again. Keep turning toward yourself. Keep doing the hard work. You've got this, and I've got you.

CHAPTER 18

LETTER TO MYSELF

"Our wounds are often the openings into the best and most beautiful part of us."

—DAVID RICHO

"Knowing what you know now as a CEO and female founder, what advice would you give to your former self?"

I closed my eyes and thought about it for a second. I was being interviewed for an upcoming magazine article, and for once I was the one needing to answer. As the host of an international podcast and speaker, I was used to holding the cards and asking all of the questions, but now the tables were turned.

My mind wandered back to a time in fourth grade when my teacher Mrs. Randall asked us to write a letter to our future self and place it in a time capsule. The plan was to bury the time capsule and dig it up at a later date. I never saw the letter I wrote again. *Now was the time for a second chance.*

I remember writing my letter with my number two pencil in my Trapper Keeper notebook. In the letter I wrote that my future self would be happily married, I would be my own boss, and one day I would write a book. There was no mention of having kids—only a dog.

After I thought about it some more, I responded: "I would say to my former self, 'You need to trust your gut and heart. Choose instinct over logic. When you come up against an obstacle, don't try to push through it or force it. Explore it and then choose the decision that feels best. Once you make the decision, just keep going and moving forward. People will try to give you all sorts of advice, so be cautious, listen to it, and marinate in the advice, but then act on what feels right—not what you *should* do. I would also tell my former self not to be afraid or fearful of mistakes, but instead, own them, examine them, share them, and move on.'"

The reporter seemed satisfied with my response, and we concluded the rest of the interview.

After the interview and my day ended, when I was lying in bed, the reporter's question resurfaced in my mind. Again, my answer felt unfinished, hollow. It bothered me. The question lodged itself in my brain cortex and wouldn't let me go. Going back to sleep wasn't going to happen. I threw my bed covers back and crept slowly out of bed in my bare feet so as not to disturb my husband, Peter, and the dog. I tiptoed slowly down the hall in my two-piece cotton pajama set from Target in the dark as the outside porch lights illuminated my path to my office. I walked over to my desk, sat down, and opened my journal. I wrote at the top of the page "Letter to Myself."

At this moment I realized I was sitting with myself like I hadn't been able to sit with myself on the bathroom floor. Now I was living the life I had wanted to, with work that brought meaning, healing, and value instead of fatigue and burnout. I was listening to myself and following my heart instead of leading with my head and the expectations of others. I felt calm, safe, and at peace.

Remembering fourteen months before, I had been on the cold bathroom floor, wanting to end my life because I was incapable of seeing a future without emotional pain. I didn't really want to end *my* life. I wanted the life I was living to end. I was trapped, exhausted, and hopeless—all because I hadn't trusted my inner self.

I pictured myself on the bathroom floor feeling hopeless and lost. I remember looking up toward the bathroom ceiling with tears streaming down my face and saying, "God or whoever is out there, please tell me what to do. I need help." As the words tumbled out of me, I remember the feeling of release—me finally putting the words out there and saying them out loud. Words I couldn't say to myself for so long for fear of failure, loss, and letting go.

Bringing myself back to the present in my peaceful office in the still of the night, it dawned on me why I couldn't let the reporter's question from earlier go. My response at the moment to the reporter was an authentic one, but it only scratched the surface of what I wanted to say. Like most interviews, we were running out of time, and they left the most profound question for the end of the interview.

I had more to say that I wanted to share with the world. It wasn't just enough to scratch the surface anymore. I needed to share with the world and people suffering from burnout *how* I learned to get up from the bathroom floor so I could give them hope and a roadmap to help guide them through their journey. The answer came to me in the form of Mrs. Randall's voice, "Write what you know, Hannah, and the words will flow."

In my moonlit office, like a time capsule from my past self, the words landed softly on the pages of my journal, little whispers of advice and snippets of conversations I had with myself and others throughout the darkest time of my life. A few words spilled out of me, and what began as a letter to my former self became a letter to *me* now and also to you.

This isn't just a book; it is a journey to find a way back to yourself. It's a map you can follow to help guide you to the extraordinary life I know is within you. Know when you read this, I am right there by your side, cheering you on and whispering: "Take the leap. Take the risk. Reach for your extraordinary life."

ACKNOWLEDGMENTS

For as long as I can remember, I have dreamed of becoming a published author, and with *Hello, Head, Meet Heart* making its debut, that dream is finally coming true.

Writing this book has been an incredible and emotional wild ride, which would not have been possible without the phenomenal support I have received from my community of peers, colleagues, friends, family, my parents—Morgan and Rick—my best friend Katie, and my husband Peter.

I'd like to thank all of the people whose voices I highlight in the book. Your bravery and vulnerability in sharing each of your stories are deeply touching and inspiring. Your voices kept me moving forward during some of the toughest days as a writer. Thank you for trusting me enough to translate your stories of resilience, courage, and hope and share them with the world.

A big thank you to my spectacular VIP Author's Community for their true belief in me and for the initial support they provided both financially and emotionally by purchasing *Hello, Head, Meet Heart* during the book presale campaign. You have no idea what it meant to me for you to take the time and purchase one, five, ten, or fifty books. I know you all have incredibly busy lives, but you showed through your actions that you believe in me and the message I am spreading out into the world. Because of this I would like to personally list your name here: Peter Skei, Betty Morgan, Richard Austin, Leslie Hay-Currie, Judi and Milt Stewart, Lisa Fogarty, Jodi Barschow, Geana Van Dessel Nagy, Matt Richards, Zenana Rose, Mary Jane Govaerts, Arin Forstadt, Ellissa Nagle, Eric Koester, Tawnya Scott, Paula Doroff, Molly Biller, Laura Knips, Anne Whitlock, Betsy Tong, Rachell Robson, Mary Beth Farkas, Anna Riedel, Pam Ford, Krista Powers, Stacey Brake, Aaron Underdahl, Katie Marshall, Amy Skei, John and Elizabeth Austin, Blair Harmon, Jessie Fan, Meagan Mangus, Cece Renick, Danielle Boris, Carol Campbell, Jennifer and James Bruce, Erin McCune, Jamie Pedrick, Sandra Gregg, Donna Star, Amy Cahoy, Maryanne Spatola, Tristan Fujita, JoAnne Solchany, Jennie Byrne, Jeanne Espinosa, Kristina Young, Tepring Piquado, Csilla Veress, Tom and Lori Austin, Jennifer Pointer, Deb Maccabee, Linda Weston, Kate and Rahim Abbasi, Abigail Adams, Ardice Farrow, Corinne Moynihan, Ellen Singer, Sarah Williams, Jennifer Draheim, Josh Berry, Aimee Evan, Morgan Dusatko, Greg and Roxanne Specht, Finn Roby, Jan and Bill MacClarence, Sophia Asghar, Laura Mount, Christopher and Marci Hartson,

Miriam Zylberglait, Hayley Nunn, Renee Schoenfeld, Christy Fawcett, Tausha Gangitano, Gail Douglas, Faye Radcliffe, Alena Anderson, Judy Shaver, Tobruk Blaine, Shannon Pfile, Sean McCarthy, Douglas Blake, Susan Hill, Peter Morreale, Peter Dobson, Kaitlin Walker, Albert Oh, Betsy and Robb Austin, Donna B. Spears, Emily Arion, Iselyn Hamilton Austin, Katie Kinley, Greg Davis, Lisa DeAngelis, John Kendrick, Katie Reed, Peter Stalick, Emily Jensen, Lisa Apple, Jim Young, Jeremy Norton, Marian (Rani) Jayasekera, Eliana Temkin, Todd and April Sheaffer, Serena Rapp, Paige Morgan, Kari Naone, Julia Sharp, Hirdesh Lal, Sally and Craig Olsen, Suvi Wesa, Gregory Manning, Sanja Uskokovic, Lori Spencer, Kitrina and Bill Kennedy, Richie Duncan, Erin Rhae Biller, Sarah Beggs, Melissa Hayden, Corrine Ranard, Casey Hettman, Tana Thomson & the Vista Capital team, Tamer Riad, Michiko Slick, Michael Barrett, Sky Wolfe, Dan Cook, Isaac Jones, Amy Hartman, Troy Banker, Kristin Kane, Elizabeth (Tess) Gadwa, Erik Austin, Wendy Scott and Brent Hedburg, Rebecca and Jasper Long, Carole Poff, DeAnna Sheehan, Todd Barth, Lori Taylor, Mark Lewis, Kristen Logan, Rachel Bell, Zandra Frame, Thubten Comerford, Hilie Calvert, Dr. Marisol Capellan, Laura Salerno Owens, Brian Burk, Chad Fast, Terri Imbach, Marcia Maizel-Clarke, Bonnie August, Joelle Osterhaus, Nicole Shaia, Xinjin Zhao, Jennifer Black, Ana Evans, Susan Green. Without all of you, this book would not have been published.

I would like to express my gratitude to my beta readers for taking the time to read the chapters of *Hello, Head, Meet Heart* and provide feedback along the way. Thank you, Peter Skei, Betty Morgan, Rick Austin, Christy Fawcett, Noel Van Dyke, Jessie Fan, Terri Imbach, Jeanne Espinosa, Emily

Arion, Katie Marshall, Ardice Farrow, Sharon Athas-Cote, John Kendrick and Carole Poff. The feedback you gave to me was incredibly detailed, poignant, and paramount and it made the book truly come to life.

A good writer never writes alone, and for that reason, I would like to acknowledge my writing community. Thank you to the Book Creator Program and my New Degree Press family: Eric Koester, Rachel Kyne, Gina Champagne, Jacques Moolman, Jim Young, Miriam Zylberglait, Jennie Byrne, Arin Forstadt, Danielle Boris, Lisa DeAngelis, and Annette Mason. Your support has been unwavering, and your kindness and generosity will always be remembered. You helped shape the dream that is *Hello, Head, Meet Heart.*

I would also like to thank my SheShatters team at Flourish Online. Thank you for your ideas, and inspiration and for juggling all of the priorities that have surfaced over the last two years. You have been with me from the beginning of this journey, and I couldn't be more grateful for you.

Lastly, I would like to thank those of you who have taken my calls at random times of the day and night to listen to my ideas, dreams, and worries. We've laughed, cried, shopped at Target, screamed, and brainstormed together during one of the darkest times in my life. Through it all, each of you held space for me in your heart and gently nudged me forward until I found my spark again. Thank you for being my fire starters. You know who you are. I love you.

APPENDIX

Introduction

Lighthouse Blog. n.d. "Key Gallup Workplace Statistics to Help You Lead in 2022." Lighthouse Blog. Accessed May 31, 2022. https://getlighthouse.com/blog/gallup-workplace-statistics-2022/#1.

Overton, Jennie. n.d. *Employee Burnout Statistics for 2022*. Limeade. Accessed July 12, 2022. https://www.limeade.com/resources/blog/employee-burnout-statistics-for-2022/.

Reynolds, Brie. 2021. "Flex Jobs, Mental Health America Survey: Mental Health in the Workplace." Flex Jobs. Accessed July 11, 2022. https://www.flexjobs.com/blog/post/flexjobs-mha-mental-health-workplace-pandemic/.

Threlkeld, Kristy. 2021. "Employee Burnout Report: COVID-19's Impact and 3 Strategies to Curb It." Indeed. Accessed July 11, 2022. https://www.indeed.com/lead/preventing-employee-burnout-report.

World Health Organization. 2019. "Burn-Out an 'Occupational Phenomenon:' International Classification of Diseases." World Health Organization. Accessed July 11, 2022. https://www.who. int/news/item/28-05-2019-burn-out-an-occupational-phenom-enon-international-classification-of-diseases.

Chapter 1
Oxford Advanced Learners Dictionary. s.v. "Ordinary." Oxford University Press. Accessed April 23, 2022. https://www.oxford-learnersdictionaries.com/definition/english/ordinary.

Chapter 2
Gul, Eisha. n.d. "34 Employee Burnout Statistics You Should Know." *Weshare* (blog). Accessed July 10, 2022. https://www.weshare. net/statistics/employee-burnout-statistics/.

My Disability Jobs. 2022. "Statistics about Employees Burnout in the Workplace—Update 2022." My Disability Jobs. Accessed July 10, 2022. https://mydisabilityjobs.com/statistics/employ-ee-burnout-workplace/.

Chapter 3
Dutra-St. John, Yvonne and Rich Dutra-St. John. 2009. *Be the Hero: You've Been Waiting For.* Martinez, CA: Challenge Associates Press.

Chapter 4
Bell, Andrea L. 2016. "What Is Self-Regulation and Why Is It So Important?" *Good Therapy* (Blog). Good Therapy. Accessed July 11, 2022. https://www.goodtherapy.org/blog/what-is-self-regulation-why-is-it-so-important-0928165.

Kornfield, Jack. 2021. "Healing Mind." Lead with the Heart. Accessed July 11, 2022. https://jackkornfield.com/healing-mind/.

Chapter 5

Burke, Mary Kathryn. 2015. "7 Questions Answered about Transgender People." *ABC News*. ABC News Network. Accessed August 20, 2022. https://abcnews.go.com/Health/questions-answered-transgender-people/story?id=30570113.

Carroll, Lewis. 1866. "The Caterpillar." Story in *Alice's Adventures in Wonderland*. 40–45. Stuttgart, Germany: Macmillan.

Ciancio, Susan. 2021. "What Percentage of Transgenders Regret Surgery?" Human Life International. Accessed August 20, 2022. https://www.hli.org/resources/what-percentage-of-transgenders-regret-surgery/.

Herman, Jody. 2022. "How Many Adults and Youth Identify as Transgender in the United States?" Williams Institute. Accessed August 4, 2022. https://williamsinstitute.law.ucla.edu/publications/trans-adults-united-states/.

Chapter 6

Tolle, Eckhart. 2004. *The Power of Now: A Guide to Spiritual Enlightenment*. Novato, CA: New World Library.

Chapter 7

Keogh, Joey. 2021. "The Truth about Tyra Banks and Naomi Campbell's Feud." TheList.com. The List. Accessed July 10, 2022. https://www.thelist.com/480594/the-truth-about-tyra-banks-and-naomi-campbells-feud/?utm_campaign=clip.

Troup, Cameron MD. n.d. "Highlander Syndrome: What Is It? Known Cases, Symptoms, Causes and Treatment." Scope Heal. Accessed May 22, 2022. https://scopeheal.com/sindrome-the-highlander/.

Chapter 8

Michael. 2020. "Emotional Numbing: Why Avoiding Uncomfortable Feelings Gets Us Nowhere." Ananias Foundation. Ananias Publishing. Accessed July 12, 2022. https://www.ananiasfoundation.org/emotional-numbing/.

Chapter 9

Brown, Brené. 2018. "In You Must Go: Harnessing the Force by Owning Our Stories." Brené Brown. Accessed May 22, 2022. https://brenebrown.com/articles/2018/05/04/in-you-must-go-harnessing-the-force-by-owning-our-stories/.

Burkhardt, Michael. 2020. "You Are Not What You Think You Are—The False Self, the Ego, and the True Self." Medium. Ascent Publication. Accessed May 22, 2022. https://medium.com/the-ascent/you-are-not-what-you-think-you-are-the-false-self-the-ego-and-the-true-self-13064f51918e.

Kazmi, Ramsha. 2021. "The 3 Faces, a Japanese Proverb Theory." *Runway Pakistan*. Accessed September 26, 2022. https://runwaypakistan.com/the-3-faces-a-japanese-proverb-theory/.

Stassinopoulos, Agapi. 2012. "Unbinding the Heart: Put Yourself on Your To-Do List." *HuffPost*. Accessed May 22, 2022. https://www.huffpost.com/entry/unbinding-the-heart_b_1244184.

Walsh, Veronica. 2020. "Inner Critic." *Therapy Blog.* GoodTherapy.org. Accessed May 22, 2022. https://www.goodtherapy.org/blog/psychpedia/inner-critic.

Chapter 10

Bloom, Noelle. 2019. "10 Signs You're Living on Autopilot." SUCCESS. Accessed May 24, 2022. https://www.success.com/10-signs-youre-living-on-autopilot/.

Teamsoul. 2018. "5 Ways to Live Consciously and What Does It Really Mean." Fearless Soul - Inspirational Music & Life Changing Thoughts. Accessed May 24, 2022. https://iamfearlesssoul.com/live-consciously/.

Tonya. 2021. "How to Live Consciously in an Unconscious World." Your Aha! Life. Accessed May 23, 2022. https://yourahalife.com/how-to-live-consciously-in-an-unconscious-world/.

Chapter 12

Rohn, Jim. 2013. "If You Don't Like How Things Are, Change It! You're Not a Tree." *Philosiblog.* Accessed August 19, 2022. https://philosiblog.com/2013/07/11/if-you-dont-like-how-things-are-change-it-youre-not-a-tree/.

Chapter 14

Allen, Madison. 2022. "What Side of the Brain Is Creative?" Daily Cognition. Hestia. Accessed August 19, 2022. https://dailycognition.com/brain-health/what-side-of-the-brain-is-creative/.

Purrington, Mr. 2020. "Carl Jung: The Dynamic Principle of Fantasy Is Play...Quotations." Carl Jung Depth Psychology. Accessed 19, 2022. https://carljungdepthpsychologysite.

blog/2020/11/09/carl-jung-the-dynamic-principle-of-fantasy-is-play-2/#.YyeSF6TMK3B.

Reyes, Miriam. 2018. "The Right Side of the Brain." The Joy of Wellness. Accessed August 20, 2022. https://www.thejoyofwellness.net/the-right-side-of-the-brain/.

Wong, Kristin. 2020. "How to Add More Play to Your Grown-Up Life, Even Now." *New York Times.* Accessed August 20, 2022. https://www.nytimes.com/2020/08/14/smarter-living/adults-play-work-life-balance.html.

Chapter 16

Wiest, Brianna. 2021. "48 Ways to Get Out of Your Own Way and Start Making Real, Lasting Change in Your Life." *Forbes Magazine.* Accessed September 2, 2022. https://www.forbes.com/sites/briannawiest/2018/05/18/48-ways-to-get-out-of-your-own-way-and-start-making-real-lasting-change-in-your-life/.

Chapter 17

Peters, Julie. 2021. "Why Lying Broken in a Pile on Your Bedroom Floor Is a Good Idea." Elephant Journal. Accessed June 15, 2022. https://www.elephantjournal.com/2011/06/why-being-broken-in-a-pile-on-your-bedroom-floor-is-a-good-idea-julie-jc-peters/.

Made in the USA
Middletown, DE
26 June 2024

56364606R00109